Countrysi Leisure

C000088372

ep EP PUBLISHING LIMITED
1978

Short-eared owl taken by the author from a hide at a moorland site in Orkney. This owl hunts by day, but is busiest during the half-light periods of dawn and dusk. *Stand camera, 220 mm lens, c.1/15 sec, f22, P1200 plate developed in Azol.*

NATURE PHOTOGRAPHY

by ARTHUR GILPIN

ACKNOWLEDGEMENTS

Acknowledgements

To Professor W. G. Arnott who not only read the manuscript of this book and made many helpful suggestions, but also gave of his valuable time to read the proofs, I am deeply indebted. Over the years K. Bass has advised upon and made for me pieces of equipment to adapt cameras for nature photography and his skill and help are greatly appreciated. My work has been influenced by my long working association and friendship with H. R. Lowes. His outstanding work, integrity and taste set me an excellent example for which it is difficult to thank him adequately. The comments and criticisms of the members of the Zoological Photographic Club and Nature Photographic Society have prevented my requiring a larger size of hat and for that I thank them. My original rather narrow outlook on natural history has been broadened by days in the field with that fine all round naturalist John Armitage. He introduced me to many things from snails to saprophites. To Heather Angel and Miss Anne Jackson, to Messrs. J. Armitage, S. G. Bisserôt and H. A. Hems, and to Drs. D. A. P. Cooke and M. C. F. Proctor, all of whose photographs add distinction to this book, I am indeed grateful.

Except where specifically credited, all the photographs in this book have been taken by the author. The cover picture, also photographed by the author, is of a black-throated diver.

ISBN 0 7158 0614 9

Published by EP Publishing Ltd., East Ardsley, Wakefield, West Yorkshire. 1978.

Text set in 10/11 pt Monophoto Univers, printed by photo-lithography, and bound in Great Britain by G. Beard & Son Ltd., Brighton, Sussex.

About the Author

Arthur Gilpin first took photographs of birds' nests and eggs over fifty-five years ago. In those days his camera was a box Brownie with a spectacle glass in front of the lens to allow photographs to be taken at short range. Later, having obtained a second-hand stand camera, he made a hide and commenced to photograph birds, in addition to the insects and flowers around his home. Gradually he began to specialise in the photography of birds and for many years photographed little else. However, during the last decade he has again extended his activities to take in many other forms of nature photography.

In 1935 he submitted photographs to The Royal Photographic Society's Annual Exhibition for the first time. Both were hung and one of them was reproduced in *The Year's Photography.* During the last war he served in the Royal Navy as a Photographic Officer and still managed to take nature photographs in off-duty hours. Upon returning to civilian life he was soon busy taking pictures and in 1950 The Royal Photographic Society awarded him its medal for his nature work. After becoming first an Associate and then a Fellow of The R.P.S., he served on the Nature Section of the committee that awards those honours and ultimately became its chairman.

His photographs have been exhibited in many countries and some are in permanent collections. They are also to be seen as illustrations in books and magazines. In 1973 the University of Leeds awarded him the degree of Honorary M.Sc. for his work in natural history photography. At present Arthur Gilpin is the Hon. Secretary of the Association of Natural History Photographic Societies.

CONTENTS

PREFACE

One of the difficulties of starting natural-history photography is knowing what equipment will be the most suitable for any particular branch. There is no perfect camera and a lot of money can be wasted on gadgets that will be of marginal, if any, value. Being well aware of these problems the author has pointed out in detail the advantages and disadvantages of many types of camera and of various forms of ancillary equipment.

It is hoped that this book will assist all those with a rudimentary knowledge of photography to take natural-history pictures. If the advice in it is followed, they will be able to do so without harming the creature, plant or habitat being portrayed. But this book is not only for beginners. Over fifty years' experience of wildlife photography has gone into it and even experienced photographers will find both interest and information in its pages. Those who work in one branch of nature photography will discover the book's usefulness when wishing to extend their activities into others.

INTRODUCTION

Up to about twenty years ago nature photographers were few in number. They used specialised techniques and as a result of showing prints at exhibitions and being members of postal portfolios, most of them knew each other. By far the most popular camera was the square bellows field camera. Adapted to take $3\frac{1}{4}$ in × $2\frac{1}{4}$ in (9 cm × 6 cm) film, it is still the best equipment for certain types of work. Because of that and because it is easier to explain certain photographic principles in relation to this rather simple type of camera, it and its uses will be described.

Gradually, certain reflex cameras that used $2\frac{1}{4}$ in × $2\frac{1}{4}$ in (6 cm × 6 cm) film became popular, as they still are with many workers. However, it was the improvements in 35 mm cameras, the availability of a wide variety of long-focus lenses to fit them, and trade-processed colour film, that led to a tremendous increase in the number of nature photographers. It is hoped that this book will assist not only those with some experience of nature photography, but also those just starting and others who have thought of doing so. It does not matter whether you only wish to photograph plants when you are out with your family, or whether you wish to spend all your spare time on the hobby—in either case you should benefit from reading this book.

Over the years nature photographers have built up a number of self-imposed rules concerned with the care necessary to obtain photographs without harming the subject, defining what constitutes a genuine wildlife photograph and deprecating certain practices considered to be unethical. In Britain, with the generous aid of the leading natural history and conservation bodies, the Association of Natural History Photographic Societies has produced *The Nature Photographers' Code of Practice*. This has been printed by the Royal Society for the Protection of Birds and can be obtained from their headquarters at The Lodge, Sandy, Bedfordshire SG19 2DL, England.

The basic principle all nature photographers should be guided by is that the safety of the subject is always more important than a photograph. Although much of what is embodied in the Code will appear within this book, in the interests of their own standards and of conservation everyone interested in nature photography is advised to have a copy.

In Britain it is illegal under the Protection of Birds Acts 1954-67 to disturb wilfully at the nest any species of bird placed on Schedule 1 of these acts. If one wishes to photograph one of these birds at the nest, a permit to do so must first be obtained from The Nature Conservancy, 19-20 Belgrave Square, London SW1X 8PY. Most countries now have laws protecting various creatures and plants. It is incumbent on the photographer, whether resident or visitor, to know whether and how the laws affect him or her.

When you follow a wayward butterfly or bird it is very easy to forget everything else, but it is important that when you are working where you cannot read the language you make sure you know what the notices mean. A friend of mine spent several days in a foreign jail and lost his films, because he had passed signs he could not read and was arrested within a military area. In any case permission should be obtained before you enter any private property.

A Few Photographic Do's and Dont's

Do, before starting on a holiday or expedition, make sure that the equipment required is in working order. I find it helpful to prepare a list a day or two in advance and check the gear item by item.

Do protect your cameras and films from very high temperatures. In hot countries the best place for film, new and exposed, is in a refrigerator.

Do, when cameras and films are out of use in places of high humidity, keep them in moisture-proof containers. Plastic boxes with snap-on lids are ideal.

Do, particularly when humidity is high, frequently check that the lens is not misting over.

Do check the moving parts of cameras frequently. When the camera is empty, open the back and, looking through it, fire the shutter at different speeds and stops. Far too often one hears of sticking mechanism resulting in wastage of film.

Do, before reloading, ensure that the interior of the camera is free from dust.

Do carry plenty of film. Considering the cost of equipment and travel, film is the cheapest part of nature photography.

Don't pack expensive and fragile cameras in luggage that may receive rough treatment or be subjected to extremes of temperature. For example, the luggage bay of an aircraft can be very cold and,

although films will not be affected, cameras may be.

Don't leave photographic gear unattended in a public place, even for a few minutes.

Don't ask a stranger to keep an eye on your gear for you. This seems obvious, but I knew a famous cine-photographer who lost all his very valuable apparatus at the start of an expedition as a result of tipping a bystander to look after it while he went to the booking office.

Don't allow films, whether exposed or not, to go through any X-ray inspection at an airport or customs post.

Don't, particularly where there is a lot of vegetation, casually put down your equipment case while you stalk a subject. I did just that stalking a butterfly on a Corsican hillside and, when I had obtained my picture, I turned to look down upon a large area of scrub of striking sameness. The next half-hour's anxious search taught me a lesson. Now, if I must leave my spare equipment while stalking in the wilds, I place it by a tree or rock that can easily be identified from a distance.

Whatever branch of nature photography you choose, remember that the more you know of your subject, the more likely you are to obtain good results. An experienced naturalist will find more to photograph than a photographer who relies on chance or information received from others. Furthermore, with knowledge one is more likely to be able to bring out the essential characteristics of the creature or plant.

Aims

When starting, one is inclined to take photographs of any and every type of natural-history subject. If your aim is to continue to do so you will require a wide range of equipment and knowledge. That is, of course, if you wish to produce more than casual random snapshots of species you cannot name. The earlier you decide just what you wish to photograph and why, the more likely you are to save money, time and temper. If you are already a botanist, lepidopterist or birdwatcher you will have a general idea of your aims, but even within one family of creatures there are many variations of approach. The equipment for photographing a bird at the nest can be very different from that required to take pictures of it in flight. Having made your decision you can begin to obtain the right equipment without purchasing unnecessary items.

When you are taking photographs remember that, although all nature photographs are records, there is no reason why many of them should not also be pictures. Before taking a photograph consider the pictorial possibilities of the subject; once the exposure has been made there is little one can do to alter the final result. Always try to find good specimens of the species you wish to photograph in attractive sites that are typical. With a common flower, for instance, you can search until you find one in surroundings that compose well. Rarities offer fewer opportunities, but even if one has to be satisfied at first with a photograph of a flower in an unphotogenic setting, one can continue searching for a better one. Whether you wish to take pictures or records, what follows should be of assistance, but it is written in the hope that you will not overlook pictorial possibilities.

SOME BASIC PHOTOGRAPHIC INFORMATION

It is possible to buy a modern camera, load it with colour film that the makers will process and take reasonably good photographs without any photographic knowledge. However, there are several fundamentals the photographer should know, even though the camera seems designed to cope with everything. Knowing the principles assists one in working out problems.

Lenses

There are three basic types of lens the nature photographer may require to use. These are the normal anastigmatic type, telephoto and mirror lenses. The last two mentioned were designed to reduce the distance needed between the lens and the film. When focused on a very distant object at infinity, a normal lens is its own focal length from the film. So, an 8 in (200 mm) focal-length lens would need to be that distance from the film. The distance varies a little; because of the variations in computation, the point of the lens from which the measurement is taken differs slightly, but for our purpose it is adequate to assume that the focal length of a normal lens is the distance it is from the film when focused at infinity. When the camera is focused on a subject nearer than infinity the lens is moved forward, the distance between it and the film increasing. This may continue until the object and the image on the focusing-screen are the same size, and the lens will then be halfway between them. The lens is then twice its focal length from the film. An 8 in (200 mm) lens camera will thus be extended to 16 in (400 mm).

It is obvious that for practical purposes there is a limit to the length one can extend a camera. As the demand for longer-focus lenses grew, it was discovered that by introducing a concave lens behind a normal type of lens, the lens-to-film distance was approximately halved. This was the birth of the telephoto lens. The standard of definition produced by the earlier models was rather poor, but the use of different combinations of lenses made of different glass has altered that. With the better-quality telephoto lenses now on the market the definition is very good.

However, even the telephoto lens did not completely solve the problem. The standard lenses for miniature cameras are usually 50–55 mm focal length and the cameras are built to give a film–lens distance of that order. When it is necessary to focus closer than infinity, the lens moves forward by means of a spiral system within its mount. With longer-focus lenses it is necessary to build the required extension into the mounting. This means that very-long-focus lenses are heavy and cumbersome. One of 1000 mm focal length may be upwards of 30 in (75 cm) long. It was because of this that mirror lenses were designed.

These are usually of 500 mm or 1000 mm focal length. Within them the light is reflected back and forth, making it possible to produce lenses much shorter and lighter than telephotos of equivalent focus. They have fixed stops, usually at f8 or f11, and do tend to over-emphasise background highlights; but they are invaluable for long-range shots. The position of the fixed mirrors inside the lens is critical and if they are disturbed by a knock, repairs can be expensive, so it pays to be particularly careful with this type of lens.

Another integral part of the photographic lens is a system for changing the aperture through which the light passes. The various apertures are known as stops and the standard numbering for them is f2.8, f4 or 4.5, f5.6, f8, f11, f16 and f22. There are others above and below, but these are the ones that concern us. These varying stops can be set on an adjustable diaphragm within the lens barrel that can be operated either manually or automatically. In a normal lens the aperture at f8 has a diameter equal to one-eighth of the focal length. For example, in an 8 in (200 mm) lens it is 1 in (25 mm). The smaller the stop number, the larger the aperture.

Few, if any, lenses give their best definition at full aperture. Very large aperture stops give little depth of field, so that most nature photographs are taken at f8, f11 or f16. There is no point, therefore, in paying extra for lenses with very large apertures. One way in which a large-aperture lens is helpful is in allowing extra light through when you are focusing. However, a lens with a maximum aperture of f4.5 will in most circumstances allow enough light for this purpose, after which you will stop down to the f8-f16 range where you will get best definition.

Shutters

Your film requires exactly the right amount of light to produce a correctly exposed negative or transparency. Two things control the quantity of light: the aperture and the shutter. The faster the shutter moves, the bigger the diameter of the stop required. At first it may appear that the best way to take a nature photograph is to use the fastest shutter speed and the largest aperture the light will allow. This would certainly reduce the possibility of movement of either camera or subject. Unfortunately, as I have said, the larger the stop the less the depth of field. The depth of field, sometimes called depth of focus, is the distance between the nearest and farthest points in critical focus. This varies with the distance of the camera from the object, the focal length of the lens and the aperture. The nearer one is to the subject, the longer the focus of the lens; and the larger the stop, the less the depth of field. For most close-ups a stop of f11 or smaller is required to ensure an adequate depth of field. It will be appreciated that a small stop resulting in less light passing through the lens will mean that the shutter must remain open longer. For some types of nature photography it is important that the shutter should have a good range of speeds below 1/25 sec. Its job is to allow in light for exactly the right length of time.

Two types of shutter are suitable for the nature photographer's use. They are the sector- or leaved-type (like the Compur), and the focal-plane.

With the sector-type the leaves open from the centre and then close. At their maximum opening a slight click is made and this may cause a sensitive creature to move during the exposure. They are synchronised for flash on all speeds. These normally range from 1 sec to 1/200 sec, although some give 1/500 sec, and are quieter than the focal-plane shutters. One sector-type of shutter that was used extensively with field cameras and which I still use on occasion is the Luc. The leaves are not opened by a spring, but by the photographer's pressure on the release. They open to their optimum, then are closed by a spring. There is no sound as the shutter opens and closes, but there is a slight click when it is closed. The photographer can open the shutter as slowly as he or she pleases and hold it open if a long exposure on a stationary object is required.

There are no speeds fixed, but the shortest exposure that can be given is about 1/40 sec. This is the ideal shutter for photographing shy creatures by available daylight.

Most 35 mm cameras have focal-plane shutters. These are made up of blinds with an adjustable space between the edges that move across close to the film, and the light through the slot exposes it. High speeds can be obtained and some of these shutters will give 1/2000 sec. However, the usual ranges offered are 1 sec to 1/500 or 1/1000 sec. Focal-plane shutters are, as a rule, rather noisy and as a result of their design can only be synchronised with electronic flash at a limited range of slowish shutter speeds. They do allow one to change the lens without fogging the film.

Films

In addition to the speed of the shutter and the size of the stop, one must take film speed into consideration when deciding upon the exposure required. There are two ways of rating the speed of film, ASA and DIN. Both are usually printed on the packet in which the film is packed. ASA is the most generally used and some built-in exposure meters are not engraved for DIN settings.

In the field, black-and-white negative films of speeds ranging from 100ASA to 400ASA are normally used. Correctly developed, the slower films give slightly better definition and less grain than do those of higher speed. When the light is poor or the subject moving, fast films give a better chance of success. Where a 100ASA film would require an exposure of 1/25 sec, one of 400ASA would only need 1/100 sec. Alternatively, if a greater depth of field was required, the faster film would allow a smaller stop to be used at 1/25 sec. It is advisable with 35 mm film to use the slowest that allows a reasonable chance of success. At the same time it is as well to be familiar with one film at each end of the speed range. Using the same films regularly one learns their characteristics and how to get the best out of them. When trying

out a new type of film follow the maker's instructions. The developers and times recommended will produce technically good negatives that you can use as a standard with which you can compare the results of any changes you make.

Colour transparency films normally range in speed from 25ASA to 125ASA. (There is one of 400ASA but I have no experience of this.) Two of the most popular are 50ASA and 64ASA and these give very good quality. Nevertheless, it is worthwhile keeping a fast film handy in case something has to be photographed in a poor light or at a high speed.

Sooner or later someone will tell you that they get good pictures by rating film at a much higher speed than the makers. You can believe them, but do not copy them; their shutters may be giving exposures that are much slower than those shown on the setting. If, however, you get consistent under- or over-exposure, the easiest way to allow for it is to decrease or increase the film rating on your exposure meter.

Field or Stand Cameras

As with many other things, one can say of negatives, the bigger the better. A correctly focused, exposed and developed $3\frac{1}{4}$ in × $2\frac{1}{4}$ in (9 cm × 6 cm) film will make larger grain-free prints with good definition, than will a similarly treated 35 mm film. For about the first sixty years of nature photography most pictures were taken with field cameras. These, substantially constructed of mahogany and brass, are also known as stand cameras, as they are invariably used on a tripod. Gradually, as lenses, materials and techniques improved, negative sizes became smaller. Starting at half-plate $6\frac{1}{4}$ in × $4\frac{1}{4}$ in (16 cm × 12 cm), they came down to quarter-plate $4\frac{1}{4}$ in × $3\frac{1}{4}$ in (12 cm × 9 cm). Then, when suitable plates ceased to be manufactured, most workers using this type of camera turned to roll-film holders and $3\frac{1}{4}$ in × $2\frac{1}{4}$ in (9 cm × 6 cm) film.

The type of camera favoured by nature photographers has square bellows that allow a camera extension of some 16 in–18 in (40 cm–45 cm). One of the great advantages of this type is that the front is fixed to the baseboard. When the camera is being focused the front remains stationary while the focusing screen moves away from it. Working in a hide, there is no difficulty in setting up the camera with its front the right distance from the front cover. With the tapered-bellows camera the lens moves forward, and when focusing is complete the camera sometimes projects too far so that a fresh start has to be made. On the front of the square-bellows camera —not usually less than 6 in (15 cm) square—there is plenty of space to mount the large sector shutters and lenses used.

One of the most important movements on this camera is not, to the best of my knowledge, available on any single- or twin-lens reflex, this is the swing back. One can, by tilting the back out of parallel with the camera front, bring extra areas into focus without changing the stop. The depth of field will not be increased, but it can be angled to include more of the subject.

When you have your field camera in a hide and have focused on bait or a regularly used perch or path or on a nest to which a bird or mammal is expected to come, you will be able to concentrate all your attention on choosing the right moment to press the release, then await the next opportunity after turning on the film.

The field camera is bulky and takes some time to set up. It is useless for creatures moving at any speed unless it is combined with electronic flash, and refocusing is a slow job. However, there is no better camera for the photography by available light of birds or mammals at the nest, of plants in situ and for certain types of controlled work.

$2\frac{1}{4}$ in $\times$ $2\frac{1}{4}$ in (6 cm $\times$ 6 cm) Single-Lens Reflex Cameras (SLRs)

Of the two types of reflexes taking this size of negative, the single-lens type is the most popular with nature photographers. With their wide choice of

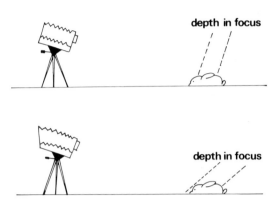

The advantage of a swing back

lenses and other accessories readily available, they are somewhat akin to the smaller 35 mm SLRs. The light passes through the lens to a mirror that reflects it on to a focusing screen. Then it is possible to view the image from above or through a pentaprism at eye level from the rear of the camera. When the release is pressed, fractionally before the shutter opens, the mirror swings out of the light path, to return when the exposure is completed. Unfortunately, the mirror movement is not soundless and as the energy needed to raise the mirror is considerable, camera vibration may be caused. When working at slow shutter speeds or close to sensitive creatures, the mirror can be locked up when focusing has been carried out. Then, using a sector-type shutter one is in the same situation as when using a field camera, although the various movements available on that camera are lacking.

With some SLRs of this size one can use either a sector or focal-plane shutter. Using the first when quietness is an advantage or with flash, and the last for flying birds and from-the-shoulder shots of animals, one has the best of both worlds. In addition, one can use lenses of longer focus with SLRs than with twin-lens reflexes of this size, and with some

A record of habitats ranging from the river to the mountains worked in Spain by a group of wildlife photographers. Bee-eaters and kingfishers nested in the bank shown at the lower left; golden orioles and azure-winged magpies along with many others were in the trees, and in the mountains there were eagles and kites. *Retina III SLR, 50 mm lens, 1/250 sec, f8, Panatomic-X film developed in Microdol X.*

These bee-eaters on a natural perch were photographed from a hide on the Spanish river bank shown opposite. *Stand camera, 220 mm lens, c.1/20 sec, f22, P1200 plate developed in Azol.*

models one can have interchangeable film magazines. These allow the photographer to change quickly from one film to another.

One problem with these and 35 mm SLRs is that whether one wishes to stalk a small creature with a long-focus lens, or to take a close-up with one of shorter focus, one has not enough focusing extension for an image of worthwhile size. There are definite limits to the distance to which the lens can be moved forward in its mount and one must introduce an extension between it and the camera to be within the range of focus if the subject is too close. The extension can be in the form of either tubes or bellows. The tubes are sold in sets of varying lengths and can be used individually or in any combination. With each one or combination, the lens will focus over a short distance and one can spend some time finding the right length for the range required. When in position, bellows allow the distance between the camera and lens to be varied at will. The bellows are much handier than the tubes, but considerably more expensive. With either, one usually loses the automatic closure of the diaphragm that is now almost standard on SLRs.

35 mm Single-Lens Reflex Cameras

Its compactness, versatility, the availability of many lenses and gadgets to fit it, and the fact that this camera can be used both for nature photography and also to take the family holiday snaps, continue to make the 35 mm SLR first choice for many.

Much of what has been written about the 6 cm × 6 cm SLRs applies also to the smaller camera. Although for the 35 mm user there are now a few lenses available specially designed to include close-range focusing, most of the lenses are not so designed and require to be used with extension tubes or bellows for close-ups.

A 35 mm SLR, if one includes second-hand values, may in 1978 cost anything from £25.00 to more than ten times as much. Therefore, much will depend on the amount you wish to spend. If funds are limited, make sure the camera you buy has a lens fitting that is popular, so that you will find it easy to purchase extra lenses.

The basic requirements are:

- the camera body should be strongly made and allow lenses to be interchanged,
- the shutter should be consistent and provide for time exposures and slow speeds,
- the lens should be of a reasonable standard.

If the shutter is a quiet one, so much the better.

Most modern 35 mm SLRs are automatic and have through-the-lens metering. Both are desirable refinements. With the automatic camera one can focus at the full aperture of the lens, set the shutter speed and stop required and when the release is pressed the aperture automatically closes to the right stop. As already mentioned this does not usually operate when extension tubes or bellows are used and the stop must then be set manually. Through-the-lens metering (TTL) allows one to take the exposure while looking at the scene in the viewfinder. By altering the shutter speed or stop, or both, one centres a needle to be seen on the edge of the frame. The camera will then give the correct exposure for what is within the field of view (see page 18 for the variations sometimes required). With some of the more sophisticated and expensive cameras the stop and shutter speed also show on the frame's edge; these are a great help. Without this advantage it pays to check the stop and shutter settings after the exposure reading has been taken, as one may have too large a stop or too slow a speed for the subject. It is then a matter of balancing one against the other, reducing the aperture and slowing the shutter speed if the depth of field is inadequate, or opening up and increasing the speed of the shutter for something fast-moving. When in a hide, it is a great advantage if you are able frequently to keep check upon the exposure through the lens, as light variations are difficult to assess when you are looking out of a small peephole.

As there is space for only a smaller image on a 35 mm film, when a 6 cm × 6 cm and 35 mm camera placed side by side are arranged so that the image of the object fits exactly in the width of the screen, the 35 mm camera will have the shorter focus lens. At any given stop it will also have a greater depth of field. If the same depth of field is obtained on both, the stop of the shorter-focus lens will be larger, and all other things being equal, a faster shutter speed can be used. The possibilities of faster shutter speeds and of a good depth of field are among the advantages of 35 mm cameras.

When you deal with 35 mm film, absolute cleanliness and care are required at every stage. Stress marks and scratches can ruin either negatives or transparencies, and the interior of the camera, as well as the film, should be treated with respect.

2¼ in × 2¼ in (6 cm × 6 cm) Twin-Lens Reflex Cameras

On account of their limited focusing range, most twin-lens reflexes are unsuitable for nature work. Only one of them, the Mamiyaflex, has achieved any popularity and some fine work has been done with it. It has quite a long extension and with it lenses up to 250 mm focal length can be used. As its name implies, this type of camera has two lenses, one above the other. The upper lens throws the image on to a fixed mirror that reflects it on to a focusing screen at the top of the camera; this can be viewed from above, or, by the addition of an accessory, at eye level. The lower lens, fitted with a diaphragm and in a sector-type shutter, takes the picture. When lenses of different focus are required, the camera front is removed and another, with matched lenses, put in its place. As one might expect, owing to the distance between the taking and viewing lenses, there are, at close range, problems of parallax. Within the camera is a bar that moves down the screen and indicates the top of the picture as the bellows are extended. For all but close-ups this is an adequate guide, but it is not so

for taking photographs at a short distance. Then an accessory that allows the camera to be lifted by exactly the measurement between the lens centres is required. This is fitted to the tripod and the camera is fixed on top. After composing and focusing in the normal way, the slide on the accessory is moved upwards and locked, placing the taking lens where the viewing lens was when focused.

The viewing lens gives a bright image on which to focus, but does not show the effect of stopping down. The depth of field is indicated on a scale at the side of the camera, but this is less satisfactory.

Exposure

No exposure meter will give the correct exposure every time and one must frequently make allowance for special conditions. This is particularly the case when reversal colour material is being used. With a negative–positive process, one can make adjustments when the print is made, but with reversal film there is no easy way of compensating for wrong exposure. Most colour films for transparencies have an exposure tolerance of no more than plus or minus one-third of a stop.

With a good-class meter, such as a Weston, either the incident or reflected light can be measured; a TTL meter measures the reflected light. The incident light is measured by placing the exposure meter, with a translucent dome over the light-receiving area, in front of the subject and facing the source of the light that falls on it. To measure the reflected light one points the meter, whether separate from the camera or TTL, at the subject. Taking the exposure by incident light is very effective with stationary subjects, particularly when they are very light against a dark background or dark in front of a light one. If an exposure based upon an unadjusted reflected light reading was made in those two circumstances, the subject in the first would be over-exposed and the second under-exposed. With such situations, if one takes a reflected light reading, it should be of the subject only, including the minimum of background. The whole may be then photographed and the main item will be correctly exposed. Another problem when using a separate meter is that as the camera lens is moved farther from the film more exposure is required. The proportion of increased exposure required for the extra extension has to be worked out and added to the meter reading. It will be appreciated that the use of a separate meter adds time to the taking of a photograph and it is mainly the photographer of plants or fungi that will benefit from its use.

With TTL metering it is reflected light passing through the lens that determines the exposure, therefore one does not require to make allowance for any extra extension or filters. Although some meters of this type are so designed that the main reading comes from the centre of the picture area, one does have to allow for wide variations between the depth of colour of the subject and background. A good example of this problem and its treatment is the photograph of the crested barbet on page 19, which was taken from a pylon hide in the Transvaal bush. I decided to photograph the bird in the shade because when sunlit the area around the nest hole was criss-crossed with shadows. The bush behind the nest was brilliantly lit and when I composed the picture on a Nikon F with TTL metering, I realised that the light background was affecting the exposure. Then, pointing the lens lower down at a broader part of the tree, I took a reading for the trunk alone. Although the meter indicated over-exposure when I directed the camera at the nest again, I made no change and the photographs, including colour transparencies, were correctly exposed. When taking a photograph of any creature against a background of sky, first point the camera lower down, but in the same direction, and take a reading from foliage receiving the same light.

With TTL metering the meter setting is based upon the assumption that the shutter is working accurately. If exposures are wrong the shutter is as likely a cause as the meter.

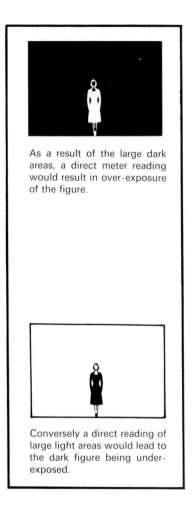

As a result of the large dark areas, a direct meter reading would result in over-exposure of the figure.

Conversely a direct reading of large light areas would lead to the dark figure being under-exposed.

Camera Supports

For taking photographs of subjects at a short distance and for working in a hide, a tripod is essential. It should be rigid, and the legs should not be a U-section; these clog when pushed into soft earth or mud, and require clearing before the telescopic legs

can be closed. The top should pan and tilt. If you are using a 35 mm camera the plate to which the camera

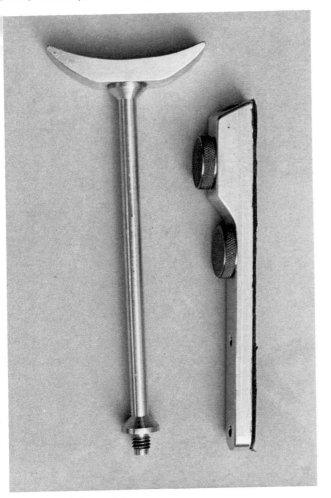

Shoulder-pod dismantled

Crested barbet (South Africa). The light reading was taken from the shadowed trunk. *Nikon, 300 mm lens, 1/60 sec, f16, FP4 film developed in Promicrol.*

is fixed must be hinged so that vertical pictures can be taken. For use with very long-focus lenses the tripod should be very sturdy.

For stalking with long-focus lenses or photographing flying birds, a stout shoulder-pod is a very useful piece of equipment. One can buy adjustable ones, but these, by their very nature, have moving parts and unnecessary pieces. I have found the made-to-measure type light, rigid and easy to carry in a bag or pocket. Having one made of light alloy should not cost much more than the price of an adjustable one (see page 19).

Camera on a shoulder-pod

Flash

While there is no doubt that daylight is the best light for taking nature photographs, sometimes, because of dark situations or the need for a very short exposure, artificial light in the flash form is required.

Two types of flash are in general use—bulbs and electronic. Bulbs are on the whole more powerful, have a longer flash—some of which is wasted when synchronised—and can be fired by simple equipment. Each bulb can only be used once so that this form of flash becomes expensive if a number of photographs are required. Changing them from inside a hide can be a great disadvantage, as one has to reach out to do so. Even if you wait for the subject to go away after the flash, you may find that it will watch from a distance and will not return if it sees your arm appear.

Although the first electronic flash was bulky and required heavy batteries, the sets are now quite compact and reasonably lightweight. Flashes are short, thus stopping movement, and there is no need to change bulbs. A ring-flash is particularly suitable for small subjects at short range. This is a curved lamp that fits around the lens and its use obviates shadows. For the same sort of subjects a compact flash that fits the camera accessory shoe can be effective. For taking photographs from a greater distance one requires more powerful sets, preferably with at least two flash heads. As the use of two heads on one set halves the speed and power of each, some workers prefer two sets with a slave unit fitted to one of them. With this system no trailing wires connect the sets, for the second lamp responds to the flash of the first. There is a wide choice of high-speed flash equipment, and your purse, your camera and the sort of photography you are interested in will determine what you buy.

In my opinion it is best to have done considerable field work and to have familiarised oneself with photography by daylight before spending money on flash equipment. You may miss some opportunities because you lack it, but by developing the more difficult technique of taking photographs by available light, you will have laid a sound foundation on which to build. If and when you do buy electronic flash equipment you will then have a good idea of what you require for your particular type of work.

Filters

For colour photography the only filter in general use is the UV (ultra violet), sometimes called a haze filter. Screwed into the lens mounting in front of the lens, it not only cuts out haze and the excess blue in seascapes or mountain views, but it protects the front element of the lens. As it does not increase the exposure it can be left permanently in position. I have not found it to be any advantage when taking photographs at short range. Unless considered to be worthwhile for the protection given against physical damage, this filter is unnecessary on lenses other than those used for photographing habitats and scenery.

Colour filters for black-and-white film have one grave disadvantage for the nature photographer, who often has the problem of getting a short enough exposure with adequate depth of field—that is, they increase the exposure required. Fortunately, present-day film is extremely good at rendering colour values in monochrome, so that colour filters have a limited use. A 2X yellow filter helps to bring out the sky in landscapes and increases the contrast between bird and sky in flight shots. If you wish to darken the sky even more, a deeper yellow or even a red filter may be used, but the exposure will increase with the extra colour depth of the filters by even as much as five or six times.

Hides

The Kearton brothers, who are the best remembered of the British pioneers in bird photography, went to extremes to make their hides look natural. In woods, they used an imitation tree trunk with ivy trailed around it; in lowland fields, an ox skin stretched over a wicker frame; in moorlands, a sheepskin similarly treated; and by the sides of becks they placed an artificial rock. All this has now been found to be unnecessary. If introduced properly, a simple rectangular tent is all that is required. The cover should be brown or green in colour and as far as the wildlife is concerned camouflage, either painted or natural, is not required. I have one commercially produced cover that is splashed with paint of different colours, but all the others are plain brown or green. It is, however, sometimes advisable to cover a hide with natural material gathered in its vicinity, to prevent it attracting unwelcome human attention.

Although some hides are built in situ, most wildlife photographers use portable hides for the larger part of their work. When not in use the frames can be dismantled and, wrapped in the cover, they can be carried quite easily. Sizes vary, but one must compromise between portability, keeping the size small enough to create the minimum disturbance to both surroundings and subject, and having enough space to carry out photography in reasonable comfort. Experience has shown that 1 yd (0.9 m) square and 5 ft (1.5 m) tall is about right. There are many designs for collapsible frames. My own choice is for one with adjustable uprights. These are a great advantage on uneven ground, and when something on or close to the ground is being photographed, the top needs to be high enough only for the comfort of the occupant. Each leg is made from two alloy tubes, one sliding smoothly within the other. At the top of the lower length is a milled-headed screw that holds the upper tube at any desired height. At the top of each leg is a brass turning rather like an inverted mushroom in shape. Three $\frac{1}{4}$ in (5 mm) holes are drilled into the flange of each to receive the bent-over ends of the iron rods that form the top frame. The stems that project upwards pass through eyelet holes at the corners of the top of the cover. To them guy cords can be attached if necessary.

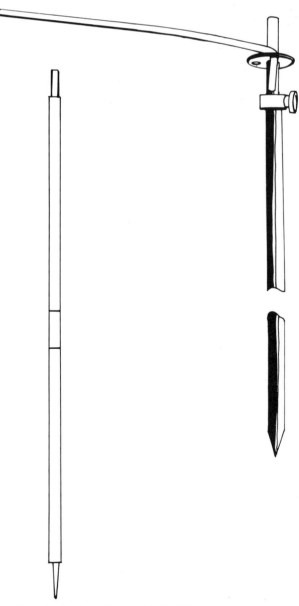

Dowel and adjustable uprights for hides

A simpler hide can be bought complete with cover. The legs are of $\frac{3}{4}$ in (2 cm) dowel, three lengths to each. A short piece of alloy tube is fixed to the top of the lower section allowing half its length above for the upper dowel to slide in. There are no spacing pieces at the top, but the legs project through holes in the top of the cover so that guys can be attached. As the guys go on after the cover, erecting this type single-handed can be difficult. Apart from that I found the one I used very satisfactory, with the added advantage of being very light to carry. An adequate frame can be made from four of the three-way corners used in some of the systems of bench and shelf erection. Into them, garden canes or dowels of the right length and thickness can be pushed. If three-way corners cannot be obtained commercially, they can be made by welding three 4 in (10 cm) lengths of electricians' tubing at right angles to each other.

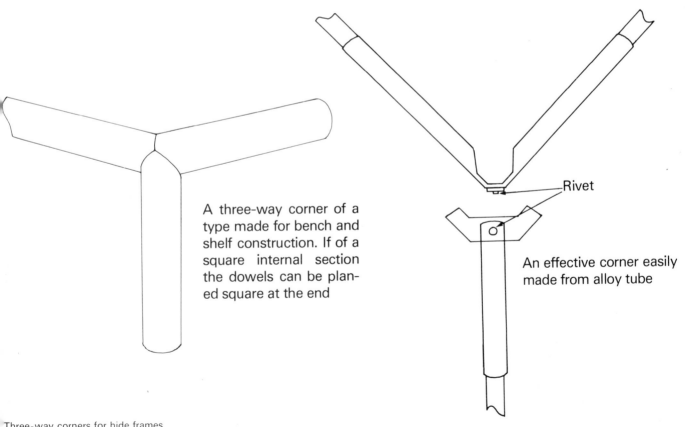

A three-way corner of a type made for bench and shelf construction. If of a square internal section the dowels can be plan-ed square at the end

Rivet

An effective corner easily made from alloy tube

Three-way corners for hide frames

It is important that the cover of a hide should fit tightly over the frame. A flapping cover may drive away the creatures that you wish to photograph and even if it does not do that, it will make them unduly

This hide was by a dotterel's nest in the Grampians, Scotland. *Stand camera, 150 mm lens, 1/25 sec, f11, P1200 plate developed in Azol.*

wary and jumpy. A hole or sleeve for the lens and peepholes are required in the cover. A sleeve should be at the centre of the front of the cover and about 9 in (23 cm) down from the top. Both the diameter at the wide end of the sleeve that is attached to the cover, and its length should be about 10 in (25 cm). The narrow end with elastic in tight enough to close it, requires to be 5 in (12 cm) in diameter. In practice the lens is pushed into the sleeve and the elastic tightens on to the lens barrel. My own choice is for a rectangular opening about 10 in × 7 in (25 cm × 18 cm) in the centre of the front some 9 in (23 cm) from the top. This has a flap of the same material inside to cover it. I have lens hoods finished with their fronts attached to pieces of cloth larger than the opening. When one works at a nest or perch, the

flap is pinned up, and after the picture is composed the hood is put on the lens and the cloth fastened to cover the space. This means that nothing protrudes beyond the front of the hide. With wait-and-see photography one requires to be able to move the camera over a reasonable arc. When doing that sort of photography I fasten elastic bands from the lower edge of the flap to the cover. That keeps the cloth close to the lens as it traverses between the lower edges of opening and flap (see page 26). Peepholes can be covered with black net or have pin-over flaps inside to adjust the size of the opening.

It is useful to have pieces of material sewn inside the hide to form pockets into which out-of-use odds and ends can be put. Also, you are advised to have the bottoms of the sides turned up about 4 in (10 cm) and fastened every 18 in (46 cm) as a receptacle for sand or stones to weight the cover down. If you have the cover professionally made it is as well to have it of waterproof material. In any case the material should be dense enough to prevent the strongest sunlight casting the occupant's shadow through it. This does not necessarily mean that it should be heavy or thick. On the advice of M. D. England, a widely travelled bird photographer, I had a cover made of a cloth used for lining jackets in order to save weight when on air journeys. This was opaque enough to be used in the glaring light of the South African sun, but would be too flimsy for use on a windy Scottish moor.

The easiest way to make a cover is to buy an adequate length of material of a suitable width (1 yd or 1 m), divide it into two halves, lay them across each other at right angles (as on page 27) so that the centres concide, sew around the square that will be the top and join three of the sides. It will be necessary to sew tapes along the open edges; they form the entrance to the hide at the back and need to be secured when the photographer is inside. Before actually sewing the whole together, you will probably find it convenient to do the work on the sides and front.

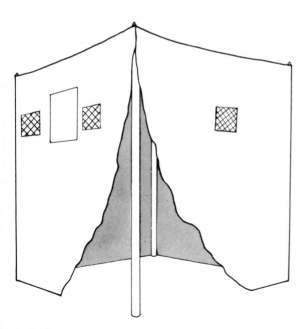

Hide details

If you are interested in bird photography at the nest, it will be an advantage to be able to build hides from which to photograph species that nest in trees. To do this you can either construct the hide in the tree or erect a pylon. It is often difficult to find a

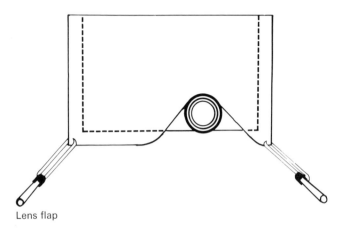

Lens flap

suitable place in a tree at just the right distance; if there is one, a platform and a hide can gradually be built upon it. Where trees are close together it is sometimes possible to find two from which the gap to the nesting tree can be spanned by poles. A platform and a hide can be built upon two such poles resting on branches just below the nest and with the other ends in adjacent trees.

Basically a pylon hide is four uprights that are cross-braced to keep them rigid. Some tubular-pole pylons erected by television and film companies at nests have cost hundreds of pounds. If you can afford or can borrow tubular scaffolding it is no doubt the best. Next for handiness is the drilled and slotted metal angle, now so widely used in workshops for the construction of shelves and stands. Otherwise, timber in the form of either poles or battens can be used. No matter what material the pylon is made out of, it should be well buttressed or guyed.

To photograph a buzzard's nest in Jutland this tree-top hide (hide and one supporting pole can be seen at the top right) was erected. *Folding camera, 75 mm lens, 1/100 sec, f5.6, Panatomic-X film developed in Azol.*

If you wish to photograph birds at nests on water you can use a boat, or better still, a flat-bottomed punt. Where possible, poles should be driven into the mud to keep the vessel stationary, and where the

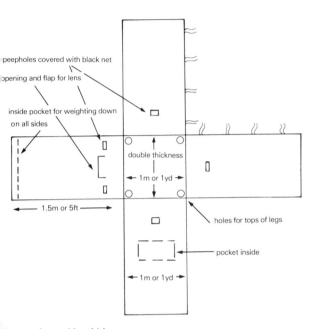

peepholes covered with black net

opening and flap for lens

inside pocket for weighting down
on all sides

double thickness

← 1m or 1yd →

← 1.5m or 5ft →

holes for tops of legs

pocket inside

← 1m or 1yd →

Pattern for making hide cover

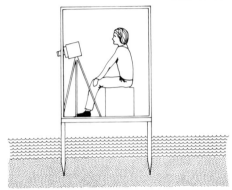

A hide on water

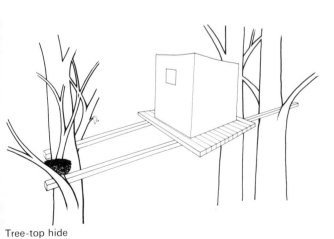

Tree-top hide

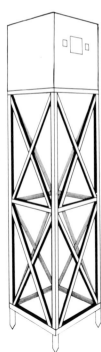

Pylon hide

water does not rise and fall a punt with a hide on it can be lashed to the poles. Unfortunately a punt is not particularly stable and where possible I prefer to build a hide from the bottom of the lake. Four poles are driven into the mud to form the corners of a square of 1 yd (0.9 m). A platform clear of the water surface is added and eventually the hide cover pulled over. This work will be done in stages, and, as soon as it is on, the platform should be weighted with heavy stones. These can be removed when the structure has settled as far as it will go. There is not much satisfaction in sitting in a slowly sinking hide.

African jacana or lily trotter from a hide in the Transvaal; the bird is walking on the surface scum that bears its weight but sinks a little under it. *Nikon SLR, 300 mm lens, 1/125 sec, f16, FP4 film developed in Promicrol.*

Remote Control

From time to time the wildlife photographer comes across situations in which for various reasons it would be unwise to erect a hide. There may be a risk of its attracting too much attention to the species you wish to photograph, or of the possibility that it will be vandalised. In such circumstances, remote control or a trip wire may be the best way to obtain a photograph. You may fire a camera at a distance by means of a length of fishing line, electricity or radio (although for the last you may require a licence from the Post Office or some other government body and in some countries it may be illegal to have such equipment). The advantage of electrical releases over fishing line is that the shutter is fired the moment the contact is made. With fishing line there is always some slack and give. However, that was the method used to take the lesser spotted woodpecker portrait on this page. Electrical releases come in various styles but all are operated by batteries and, with a little electrical knowledge, are fairly easily made. Whichever release you use, make sure that the camera is firmly enough fixed to avoid risk of vibration.

As this book goes to the printer, I have been informed that a battery-operated ultrasonic remote camera control has become available. It is made in two models, one to screw directly into the release socket, the other to fit the accessory shoe on the camera. The energy is supplied by a dry cell and the maximum working distance is 13 yd (12 m). Up to that range all one has to do to fire the camera is to point the energiser at the receiver and press the switch. As it is not radio operated no licence is required.

I have not as yet handled one of them, and the range is short for much nature photography, but I think this type of release has possibilities. Using a

Remote control was used to obtain this photograph of a lesser spotted woodpecker. The camera was fixed in the vicinity of the nest and a length of fishing line used to release the shutter, from a distance. *Stand camera, 155 mm lens, 1/20 sec, f16, P1200 plate developed in Azol.*

car as a hide, one could easily trigger off a camera placed near a feeding place or one in a place where a normal hide could not be built.

A trip system is useful for nocturnal animals and can be either cotton stretched across a path or a switch, hidden beneath leaves or grass, that makes a circuit when trodden upon. All these systems need to be made to suit the shutter of the camera used.

MAMMALS

Stalking

There are three main ways to photograph the larger mammals: stalking, baiting for them, or going to the places where they breed. Stalking may be carried out on foot, but with big game, photographs are usually taken from a vehicle. For this type of photography, a single-lens reflex used at eye level is the ideal instrument. With a 35 mm camera a 300 mm lens will probably be the most useful, with one of 135 mm for very large animals and shorter distances. For a 6 cm × 6 cm reflex a 300 mm lens and one of about 500 mm for long shots are a good combination. In neither case should the standard lens for the camera be left behind. It will be needed for habitat shots and sometimes for herds of animals.

If you are fortunate enough to have the use of a Land Rover you may be able to fasten some form of camera support to the frame. If not, you can use the window of a car. With the camera already on a shoulder-pod the window can be set at the required height, the lens rested on top and the photograph taken. Although in emergency the edge of the glass can be used, it is preferable to have something softer for the camera to rest upon. A bean bag is carried by some photographers, but a small cushion or long, narrow polythene bag filled with sand will do. Whatever is used can be fastened inside the car to prevent it falling out, and lifted into position as required. One thing to remember is that before any

photograph is taken, the engine of the vehicle should be switched off to prevent vibration. When using a shoulder-pod avoid being tense; focus, compose hold your breath briefly and fire.

In many game parks you will not be allowed either to leave the car, or take the car off the road; in these circumstances what you photograph will to a certain extent be a matter of luck. See that the vehicle is

Feeding in the sun and shadows of the Transvaal bush, this impala was photographed from a car. *Nikon SLR, 300 mm lens, 1/250 sec, FP4 film developed in Promicrol.*

driven slowly and keep alert. When the opportunity of taking a photograph is seen, you should slow the vehicle down to a stop at the roadside closest to the animals. It will then be possible to weigh the situation up and decide whether it is necessary to move nearer. Keep movement within the car to a minimum and just before taking the photograph ask everyone in the car to be still.

The steenbok is one of the smaller bucks of the bush; this photograph was taken in South Africa from a car. *Nikon SLR, 300 mm lens, 1/250 sec, f16, FP4 film developed in Promicrol.*

It is unlikely that you will be able to choose the angle of light, therefore it is advisable to set the shutter and stop, after taking average readings. Then if you are using a through-the-lens meter, you can make an adjustment before pressing the release. If you are using a separate meter, it is better to take a shot at the average decided upon; then if the animal stays, take a meter reading in case another photograph is required. It is very pleasant to photograph big game, but of recent years East African animals have been rather overdone. Editors receive many more photographs of giraffes than they do of the common house sparrow. This being the case, look out for something a little different; for example, in the photograph on page 32 the impala emphasises the great height of the giraffe. Pictures of monkeys or baboons can often add humour to a set of photographs, but when taking them be ready to close the window quickly. These animals are extremely nimble, inveterate thieves and can be in and out of a car quickly. By the roadside in the Kruger Park I saw a baboon waving some bright material that looked suspiciously like a lady's undergarment.

Stalking animals on foot is a very different matter, and it is much more difficult to stalk a truly wild deer than it is to photograph a pride of lions bemused by petrol fumes. Sound fieldcraft and a knowledge of the habits of the creature are essential, as is plenty of patience. First, one must find where the animal feeds or drinks and where it is at what time of day. Then, by stalking upwind in clothes of subdued hue and taking advantage of the cover available, you may get close enough to obtain a photograph. An alternative is to stand in cover at a place to which the animal may be expected to come, but there is then the risk of it passing downwind and scenting you. A 35 mm SLR with 300 mm lens, used on a shoulder-pod, is about the best equipment, but you may have to use lenses of longer focal length.

The giraffe and impala were photographed from a car in South Africa by the first rays of the sun at dawn. *Nikon SLR, 135 mm lens, 1/125 sec, f16m FP4 film developed in Promicrol.*

Baiting

The fox cubs shown on page 33 were photographed at bait. As the entrances to the earth were beneath bushes and surrounded by them, the only hope of photographing the cubs was to get them into a clearing that was close by. After leaving bait in the centre of the open ground for several days, I started photography. Unfortunately the earth was in a place where a hide would have attracted too much attention.

Therefore, I sat beneath the bushes on the edge of the clearing, with the camera before me on a tripod. My clothes, including gloves, were dark coloured. Knowing that there would not be enough normal light for a photograph when the cubs emerged, I had a PF5 flashbulb on the camera. I focused on the bait and, having made the necessary adjustments, sat back to wait. About half an hour after sunset I saw three cubs in the bushes and watched the vixen leave to hunt. Within minutes a cub came to the bait. The

These English fox cubs were attracted to bait. *Nikon SLR, 300 mm lens, one PF5 flashbulb, f11, FP4 film developed in Microdol-X.*

flash frightened off the cubs and I did not see them again that night. The next night I got three exposures, and eventually the cubs became so used to my presence and the flashes that they ignored both. Photographs in both black and white and colour were taken. A 35 mm SLR with a 300 mm telephoto

A badger photographed at the crossing of two regularly used paths. *Stand camera, 220 mm lens, open shutter, one flash, f22, P1200 plate developed in Azol.*

and a field camera with a 220 mm normal lens were used. Both produced satisfactory results.

Bait can be put out regularly to attract animals to come to the same spot daily, so that photographs can be taken from a hide. Alternatively a hide can be erected at a drinking place. In countries where wild carnivores roam free, that sort of thing should be done only in co-operation with someone like a game warden. One hazard is that in hot countries a snake might seek the shade of the hide.

One does not require a hide to photograph badgers; a similar technique to that used for the fox cubs is adequate. Bait ranging from kippers to chocolate has been used to attract them to chosen spots or to encourage them to climb on to a fallen tree. However, most photographs are taken near the entrance to the sett. The best position for taking pictures is slightly to the side of the entrance, where the badger cannot see the photographer until its head is clear of the hole. It should be facing any wind there is—for badgers have extremely keen scent—and backed by trees or bushes to prevent the animal seeing a clear silhouette. A badger's vision is not particularly good, but it is quick to see movement. Both its hearing and its sense of smell are acute. Once Brock's nose has appeared, silence and stillness are of the utmost importance.

Usually the preparations, focusing on the place where it is anticipated that the animal will be, and stopping down to get the right depth of field, etc., are made before sunset. Then the photographer sits close to the tripod and waits for the animal to come out. Either bulbs or electronic flash can be used, with either one or more heads. Badgers make very well-defined paths and the photograph on page 34 was taken where two of these crossed. The method was exactly as for work at the sett.

Seals breed in colonies, often on islands or remote shores. When you first land from the boat many of the adult seals will make for the sea, but if you sit down quietly they will soon return. Then, if you move slowly and make little disturbance, you will find it possible to approach them. Most of the cows will remain with their calves and some of the bulls may even charge at the photographer. The seals can be photographed with any of the cameras described, using lenses of medium focus—for example 135 mm for 35 mm and 200 mm for 6 cm × 6 cm film. The photograph on page 36 of the grey seal and cub—this is the rarest of the world's seals—was taken with a field camera on a December day when the light was poor, as is often the case when these animals are breeding.

It is possible to call up animals. Richard Kearton could attract rabbits and some people can call up hares. Trackers and game wardens often know how to decoy certain mammals. Although I do not know of anyone using the playback technique described on page 54 to attract mammals, that too has possibilities. It would be worth exploring any of these methods to aid one to obtain shots in the wild.

Small Mammals

Where they are fed regularly in public parks or private gardens some small mammals become very tame. In America, chipmunks in a small Pennsylvania garden came to be fed when the lady of the house appeared, and in England some park squirrels will take food from the hand. In such circumstances it is comparatively easy to obtain photographs. However, those who wish to photograph small mammals in the wild state require a great deal of patience. Comparatively few wildlife photographers become expert at taking pictures of such creatures as mice, shrews and voles. There are many reasons for this. Most of these species are nocturnal in habit, timorous and have extremely quick reactions. In the wild that is the only way they can stay alive, as they are the prey of many larger creatures from owls to cats. All this must be kept in mind when you prepare to photograph these mammals, but before thinking of photography you will require to learn something of the habits and haunts of the creatures to be portrayed. Reading

The rarest of the world's seals are the grey seals; this cow and calf were stalked at one of their breeding places on the British Coast. *Stand camera, 220 mm lens, c.1/10 sec, f16, P1200 plate developed in Azol.*

about them can provide a start, but eventually you must gain experience by searching and watching. The late John Markham, who did some very fine work in this field, told me that throughout the whole of one spring he spent nights watching one species so that he could photograph it the following year.

To photograph these creatures it is usually necessary to know their home or to attract them to bait. H. A. Hems, who has produced very fine photographs of many British mammals, has photographed some of the smaller species at bait in his own garden. When I tried to do similar work in a large garden in the inner suburbs of a big city, cats and birds soon discovered the bait and ate it. The presence at night of cats from surrounding gardens probably kept the rodents away. Although less than three miles from the centre of a city of more than half a million people, I found that a fox had an earth under the bushes of a shrubbery. It was only used occasionally, the fox arriving in the early morning and leaving at night, but even so its presence may have affected the animals I hoped to photograph.

However, if you have a garden which cats are not likely to invade, it is probably the best place to start. It may be that there are field mice in a rockery from which they can be tempted out in daylight by pieces of apple placed near the entrances of their tunnels. You can erect a hide, or you may decide to operate a remote camera control from a garden shed or greenhouse. The reactions and movements of such species are so quick that even in daylight the best lighting is electronic flash and a shutter of the sector type the most suitable, although any of the cameras used for bird photography should produce good results. If you wish to try baiting for small nocturnal animals, it is easier to do so if the feeding place is within easy reach of your door. Then it will be possible to put food out late in the evening and check how much has been taken early next morning. The bait should be placed at the top of some eminence—already there or introduced—to ensure that the creature to

be photographed will be clear of the surrounding grasses. When the bait is being taken regularly, the hide, with a dummy reflector sited where each flash head will be, should be placed in position.

Whether you use one, two or more flash heads is a matter of taste, but some of the most successful pictures I have seen of this type of subject have been taken with only one. At close range, electronic flash is to be preferred to bulbs. Not only is the exposure shorter, but with bulbs there is considerable disturbance every time one that has been fired has to be replaced.

One of the obvious difficulties of taking photographs of a small creature at night is to see whether the subject is in the desired position. At one time a low-power red lamp was kept burning in a position where it would illuminate the baited area, but not the hide. It was generally assumed that the animal's eyes did not register the red end of the light range. Some workers experimented and found that as long as it burned steadily and was not switched on and off, a low-powered white light was accepted. If a light is to be used it should be introduced along with the hide so that whatever comes for food would become accustomed to it. The lamp can be battery-operated or, if near a house, an extension from the mains supply and low-wattage lamp can be used. With the last method it is essential to make sure that there are no places where rainwater can enter and cause an electrical short.

The techniques of photographing small mammals close to or leaving their homes are basically the same, but the work will often be in woodlands or by hedgerows. As one cannot re-focus after dark it is advisable to have a session in the hide watching the animals' behaviour and deciding upon the area where the best chances are likely to be offered, before starting photography.

When photography starts, the camera should be focused, stopped down to get the required depth of field, and all the other preparations made in daylight.

These should be completed, with as little disturbance as possible, about half an hour before dusk. You can then enter the hide and, having made sure that you can see in comfort the area to be photographed, settle to wait. After photographing any nocturnal creature, you should make your withdrawal with as little disturbance as possible. A bright light being flashed around may spoil your chance for future sessions at the site. When preparing, consider how your equipment can most easily be broken down into separate units that, in the dark, you can carry some distance from the hide to dismantle. Also decide upon the route to be taken, to obviate the risk of tripping over obstacles such as trailing briars.

Bats are mainly nocturnal and although in theory it may appear easy to photograph them when they are asleep, to stand any chance of doing so the photographer must now a great deal about them. Considerable knowledge is required to find their sleeping and hibernating places and these are frequently difficult of access. Although on rare occasions I have found bats sleeping under loose bark or similar places, most do so in hollow trees, roof cavities and caves. Owing to their darkness, wetness and the unevenness of their floor, the last mentioned should not be entered without a companion. The humid conditions inside make the misting over of lenses a constant problem.

Most workers in this field use a single-lens reflex with electronic flash and focus by the light of a torch. However, they are aware of the dangers of too much disturbance and learn to work quickly.

Although bats have been photographed flying free and wild, the most impressive photographs I have seen of them in flight have been taken in controlled conditions by S. C. Bisserôt. For this highly specialised work he chooses a bare room with as few hiding places as possible. Photographs are taken by electronic flash which, with the camera, is triggered when the flying bat breaks a beam projected across the room. (See photographs on pages 40 and 41.)

Wild wood mice attracted by nightly baiting over a long period and photographed by H. A. Hems. *Home-made field camera, 210 mm lens, electronic flash, f16, P1200 plate, developed in D76.*

Controlled Conditions

Most wildlife photographers look upon their hobby as a field sport and find as much pleasure in pitting their wits against a wild creature's as they do in the final result. However, there are times when, because of the rarity of a creature, there is no justification for disturbing it in the wild, or else one may wish to take a series of photographs that cannot be obtained if the animal is free. It is then that controlled conditions will enable the records to be obtained. With the larger mammals this usually means going to a zoo, but smaller creatures can be photographed in captivity in the home or studio.

Although there has been a great improvement in the surroundings in which creatures are kept in zoos, one of the photographer's problems is still that

Hedgehog wandering in a wood, Yorkshire. *Stand camera, 220 mm lens, c.1/15 sec, f16, P1200 plate developed in Azol.*

of finding a reasonably satisfying background. Perhaps that is why some of the most able of those who take photographs in zoos have specialised in close-up portraits. However, at many zoos water-loving creatures like penguins, otters, sea lions and seals offer good opportunities.

Almost any hand-held camera is capable of producing photographs of animals confined in zoos, but a single-lens reflex is the most suitable. With 35 mm film a lens of 135 mm focal length will be the most useful, although one of longer focus will be required for some portraits.

In many countries there are wildlife parks in which animals have fairly large areas to range over while the visitors remain in their cars or are driven around in an estate vehicle. Apart from the fact that the animals are captured and kept in a limited area, the method of photography is similar in practice to that already described for big game. At some of these parks there are rarities that the average person would never have the opportunity to see and photograph in the wild.

With smaller creatures you can arrange the surroundings at home, taking care that they are similar to the natural habitat of the species being photographed. The animals may be captured for the purpose of photography, or be some that are kept in captivity. In either case, the photographer should know how to feed and handle them and how to make sure that they come to no harm. To minimise the risk to them, caught animals should be kept for as short a time as possible. It is advisable therefore, to have everything arranged in advance so that when the animal is caught only a few finishing touches, such as the addition of live plants, are needed. Most small mammals are confined within glass tanks while they are being photographed. An appropriate background —with no cavities in which the creature can hide— can be built at one end. Photographs can be taken over the top edge or through the glass. When you are taking photographs through the glass, the lights

Mouse-eared bat (*Myotis myotis*) photographed by S. C. Bisserôt, using high-speed electronic flash.

should be arranged so that they are not reflected within the angle of view of the lens used. By using ordinary tungsten lamps and moving them around while a check is made through the camera, you can decide upon the position for the flash heads. Although work can be done by daylight or flashbulb, electronic flash is the most suitable illuminant. In certain lightings the camera or the photographer's

Greater horseshoe bat (*Rhinolophus ferrum-equinum*) photographed by S. C. Bisserôt.

Indian smooth-coated otters, asleep. This type of photograph is extremely difficult to obtain if the animals are wild and free, but is comparatively easy to take, as here, in a zoo. *Nikon 35 mm SLR, 135 mm lens, 1/125 sec, f11, FP4 film developed in Microdol-X.*

hands will be reflected in the glass at the front of the tank. To avoid this a black card with a hole in it for the lens to go through should be fixed in front of the camera; although in my own home I have found it easier to work behind a large focusing cloth suspended on cords and with a lens hole in the centre.

As you can focus on the area where the creature will be, a field camera, with its long extension and with a shutter that can be synchronised at fast speeds and swing back, is ideal for this type of work. In addition, single- and double-lens reflexes have been employed effectively. When the photographic preparations have been made, the animal should be put in the tank and a glass sheet placed on top. The glass sheet will require a little packing beneath the corners to allow air to enter.

The creature should be allowed to settle before any photographs are taken. This may take time, but waiting is well worthwhile. A picture of an obviously disturbed animal arouses emotions other than pleasure. Movement close to the tank and noise in its vicinity should be kept to a minimum. Often it will be possible to use shorter focal length lenses than would be required to photograph the species in the wild.

In concluding this sub-section on the photography of animals in captivity, I must point out that, although is is usually easier than wildlife photography, it can be difficult. To be successful you need patience and genuine care for small mammals. Controlled photography is recognised and respected as the best method of taking certain types of picture, some of them unobtainable by other means, but the results should never be passed off as being taken free and wild.

Recommended Reading

Wildlife Photography, Eric Hosking and John Gooders (Hutchinson).

Natural History Photography, Ed. D. M. Turner Ettlinger (Academic Press):
  Section 2, John Reynolds
  Section 3, Harold Hems
  Section 1, Sdeuard C. Bisserôt.

BIRDS

There is no doubt that the photography of birds is now the most popular and the fastest-growing section of nature photography. There are many reasons for this; the main one is that the interest in birds that has been increasing steadily for many years has accelerated over the last two decades, and in almost every country the number of birdwatchers has multiplied dramatically. There has always been a percentage of those interested in birds who have wanted to take photographs of them and the law of averages indicates a proportional increase in their numbers. But that is not the whole story: 35 mm cameras with long-focus lenses can easily be carried in the field and more and more birdwatchers began to use them as recording tools, as well as a means of producing illustrations for lectures. Whereas forty years ago a bird photographer was something of a rarity, now almost any small group of bird-watchers has at least one in its number. As most bird photographers take their pictures away from the nest, I shall deal with that aspect first. All too often at a lecture on birds one is told 'that brown blur at the right is a rufous bush chat' or something similar. Transparencies should illustrate and unless the species portrayed can be recognised by those who know it, the slide conveys nothing to those who do not. As the difference between a good and a poor slide is often a matter of technique the following should help.

Birds Away from the Nest—Stalking

There is no doubt that the most suitable camera for this type of photography is the single-lens reflex. The 35 mm camera is considerably smaller and lighter than the 6 cm × 6 cm size and this also applies to the proportionately shorter focus lenses used. When you are working close to a base or car this may not be important, but after a mile or two over rough ground the difference in weight is noticeable. Through-the-lens metering is an advantage, but not a necessity. Often it is not possible to use a tripod, so a shoulder-pod is a considerable help. Sometimes a long thumb-stick is suggested as a method of steadying the camera, but then one of your hands is fully occupied holding the lens to it. With a shoulder-pod one hand can be on the pistol grip while the other focuses. If, however, there is a branch, wall or rock upon which the camera can rest during exposure so much the better. The focal length of the lenses required depends on three things: the size of the bird, the closest that the photographer is likely to be able to approach the bird, and the ability to hold the camera steady. The last varies from person to person; for instance, Brian and Shiela Bottomley, Britain's outstanding exponents of this type of photography, have successfully used a 1000 mm lens from the shoulder. Therefore, it can be seen that any focal length from 135 mm to a 1000 mm may be used, but if you are limited to a single lens, one of 300 mm to 400 mm is the best average.

The stalking techniques described on page 32 should be followed. All movements should be deliberate and slow. A bird is more likely to accept a

A great blue heron stalked away from the nest at the Brigantine Wildlife Refuge near Atlantic City, USA. *Pentax SLR, 400 mm lens, 1/250 sec, f8 on Tri-X film developed in Microdol-X.*

direct approach than a sudden appearance from behind a bush. So, if you have approached through cover, try to get into position for taking the photograph without leaving it. In the open, I have often found that setting a course that would take me past rather than to the bird has paid dividends. On the mudflats with a colleague, I have stalked birds in a way I have never seen described. Aiming directly at the bird, you start walking and stop after a few steps; your colleague follows in your footprints, and walks up to

Like puffins, black guillemots gather in parties on rocks by the sea; these were stalked in Orkney. *Mamiyaflex twin lens reflex, 180 mm lens, 1/125 sec, f22, Tri-X film developed in Microdol-X.*

you. Then you take a few more paces and your colleague follows, the action being repeated as often as required. The number of steps in each move is reduced as you get closer to the bird, until they are down to two or three. As long as a straight line is kept, whichever of you is stationary tends to mask the other's movements. I have not as yet used this method for photography, but at the first opportunity I intend, as second mover, to give it a trial, resting the camera on the leader's shoulder.

If there is a wind blowing, be careful not to wear or carry anything that will flap. Birds will take off into the wind, so, if the lighting is satisfactory from that direction, work downwind. There is no risk of birds picking up your scent.

As soon as you are close enough to the bird you are stalking to get a minimum usable image, take a photograph. This is an insurance against it taking flight when you approach closer. Continue shooting as you proceed with your stalk. As already said, film is comparatively cheap, and it is better to have a few frames you do not use than to miss the subject. In any case, it is always worthwhile making several exposures on something you may not have the opportunity to repeat. You can choose the best one for use and it always helps to have reserves in case anything happens to it. Furthermore some exposures may be spoiled by movement, either of the bird or the camera.

To avoid camera shake when you are taking pictures with the camera on a shoulder-pod, the exposure should not be longer than 1/125 sec—it should be shorter if possible—and the camera must be steady. For me the best method of holding the camera still is that first described by Mr and Mrs Bottomley. They recommend that, after focusing and making adjustments to shutter speed and stop, the camera should be lowered from the eye, the muscles relaxed, the camera brought into the taking position and the exposure made with the minimum delay. Holding a position too long brings on trembling that cannot be controlled.

If a bird is exceptionally approachable and only flies away from where it is feeding when under considerable pressure, do not harass it. These are the symptoms of a tired and hungry migrant. If prevented from feeding by constant pursuit, it could die quickly. There is no doubt that this has happened when migrants—particularly rarities—have been relentlessly chivvied by birdwatchers and photographers.

Birds at Drinking and Feeding Places

In dry areas the best way of getting pictures can be to take photographs of birds at drinking places. The smaller the area of water the greater your opportunities are likely to be. Excellent results have been achieved at a hole in a farm road that the photographer filled with water every day. It was surprising the number of species that came to what was little more than a small puddle. At larger ponds it is advisable to encourage the birds to drink at one place. One way to do this is to fix a branch on which the birds can alight and then walk down it to the water. If the water is shallow they may bathe and use the perch as a preening place. Small birds will appreciate a stone placed in the water close to the edge.

In the northern hemisphere, if you want to take photographs by daylight the hide should be erected to the south of the pond. If flash is to be used this is not so important. The distance from the pond or perch depends on the size of birds to be photographed and the focal length of the lenses to be used. Changing lenses in the hide and having to withdraw one, then put the other in its place, can easily cause the birds to fly away. It is better to set up the hide for the larger birds you are expecting and then at a later date move it forward for the smaller ones. If you are using a single-lens reflex camera, another good reason for having two hide positions rather than changing lenses is that to photograph small birds you are likely to need extension tubes or bellows. You may find it frustrating to have birds before you that are either too close or too far away to photograph, but it is even more so when the best thing of the day arrives while the lenses are being changed. As a guide to distance it is suggested that to photograph a bird that is 16 in (40 cm) long, on 35 mm film with a 200 mm lens, or on 6 cm × 6 cm with a 300 mm lens, the hide should be some 15 ft (4.5 m) away from the place where the bird is expected. Once the hide is in position, secure and with the cover tight, it should be left for at least a day so that the birds can become familiar with it. Cattle and horses can completely destroy a hide very quickly, so if any have access, or are likely to have, to the place where the hide is, it will need some form of protection. Stakes driven into the ground with barbed wire round them should minimise the risk of damage, but make sure that the fence is far enough away to prevent the animals reaching the hide with their heads, and that wires do not cross the camera's field of view.

Any of the cameras already mentioned are satisfactory for this type of work. When working at 15 ft (4.5 m) in order to get the best angle, the lens will be about 40 in (1 m) from the ground, and the camera will be near the top of the hide. It is difficult to look down into a camera in this position. 6 cm × 6 cm reflexes are easier to focus if they are fitted with a pentaprism or mirror accessory. Whether flash is used will depend on the available light and personal choice.

Photography can start when the birds are familiar with the hide and coming to the pond freely.

The back of the hide can be pinned up out of the way and the tripod set up at the front. It is important that the tripod should be rigid, so the points of the legs should be pushed into the ground. If a field camera is being used to photograph birds on a perch, it can be put on the tripod and directed at the rock or branch. With the shutter open and the lens at its largest stop, focusing can be carried out. The best way to do this is to get a colleague to hold a cigarette packet, or a card with lettering of several sizes on it, in

the position where you hope the bird will perch. Then you focus on the packet; stopping the lens down to the aperture required and still looking at the focusing screen, you ask your friend to move the packet forward. When the image on the screen begins to soften, you call a halt. You can then get an idea of how far in front of the branch the bird can project and still be in focus by looking through a peephole. When you repeat the operation behind the perch, you will find that the card moves a greater distance before going out of focus and that you have a fairly accurate idea of the depth of field. You can then close the shutter, place the roll film holder in position and find a place for your folding stool, from which you can see the perch and reach the camera. Then your assistant fastens the back and departs. All you have to do now is to wait for your opportunity and when the bird is in a satisfactory pose within the prepared depth of field, press the release.

With a single-lens reflex camera much of the procedure is the same and in fact, for photographs of the bird on the perch, it can be used almost exactly as the field camera. With a few makes of single-lens models by pressing a button you can see the effects of stopping down. However, with most makes, the depth of field cannot be determined visually and with these, it is best to focus on the front of the perch. With experience the effects of stopping down can be judged. As already mentioned if there is provision for locking up the mirror, you should take advantage of this; then you are in the situation already described, of being able to concentrate on the bird.

It is when you are working on a small pool or a short length of shore that the single-lens reflex camera comes into its own. Sitting behind the camera and looking through the viewfinder, you can move the camera over a short arc, focus and expose. When starting for the day, make sure that nothing unsightly has been dropped or blown into the area you are photographing. If left it will be an eyesore in any pictures taken. At the end of the day leave everything tidy, tight and secure.

A slight variation that can be worked is when photographing swallows or martins collecting mud for nest-building. They may do this by small road puddles or the edges of rivers and lakes. However, they do tend to move from one place to another as supplies run short or better sources are found. When these birds are seen collecting nest material, photography should start without too much delay. As

Blackcock 'lekking' in Scotland, from a hide. From March until June the blackcocks meet at dawn on their tourney grounds. *Pentax SLR, 135 mm lens, 1/30 sec, f16, Tri-X film developed in Microdol-X.*

A cock house sparrow photographed from a hide near a bird table visited by several species and quite close to the house in a small garden. *Stand camera, 220 mm lens, c.1/10 sec, f16, Iso-zenith plate developed in Azol.*

these are small, short-legged birds, the camera will be fairly close, so to avoid a plan view, keep the viewpoint fairly low.

A very different way of photographing birds away from their nests is to portray them at places where they congregate for display or combat. The males of several grouse species and some waders like the ruff, have their tourney grounds where in spring they meet intent on both activities. In suitable circumstances others, like the redshank, have mating gatherings. Many years ago, from a hide by a drying-out sewage bed, I tried to photograph the birds at one of the last mentioned. As I was using a stand camera and had to wait for the birds to come into the area upon which it was focused, I did not take many photographs. Because of the slow speeds of the plates then available, the shutter speed was not quick enough to stop movement and most of those taken were unsharp for that reason.

More recently, using modern 35mm equipment on blackcock I fared rather better. The hide was placed in the middle of one of their tourney grounds—known as leks—that had been used for several springs. As the hide was built on a windy hillside in March and was to stay in position for two or three months, the friends who erected it drove the strong uprights well into the ground. It was in April that I first used it and when storms of sleet swept across the hillside I appreciated the frame's strength and the still waterproof, but old, tarpaulin used to cover it.

The cocks come to the lek before dawn and it is in the early hours that there is most activity. It pays to be in the hide early, but I found that if birds were on the ground before me, they flew off as I walked up the hill; but were back by the time the camera was in position. Through-the-lens metering is a great asset, as one is compromising all the time between a shutter speed that will stop movement and a stop that will allow adequate depth of field. I found that in order to get feather texture in my black-and-white photographs of these birds, it was necessary to rate the film at half the speed printed on the packet.

There were about 20 cocks at the lek I worked, but some have more and others less. The contests took place as far away from the hide as 40 yards and as close as a few feet. Sometimes, in the heat of battle, the birds actually bumped into it. On a 35mm camera, lenses of 135mm and 200mm focus proved satisfactory and anything between would have done. There are moments when, prior to attacking each other, the cocks are reasonably still and these are the times to expose. The periods when one has adequate light are comparatively short, for by 8 a.m. birds begin to wander off to feed and the lek is likely to be completely deserted an hour later. At this season there will also be mornings in the hills when snow, sleet, rain or wind make photography impossible. When everything goes well it is a mistake to economise on film.

An obvious way to photograph feeding birds is to do so at a bird-table in winter. Unfortunately, it is seldom possible to get satisfactory pictures this way, as a board covered with scraps of food is not very photogenic. However, with care, you can portray birds near, but not on the food platform. Arrange a branch close to and slightly higher than the feeding place and, from the hide, you can take portraits of the birds that alight on it. For an example of what can be done in the corner of the garden see page 50. If the table is set up for photographic purposes, be sure to choose a satisfactory background to the perch. An alternative is to place food on a stone or in a cavity in an old tree stump; these will look natural in your photographs. Using equipment as described on page 47, the hide-to-subject distance of some 6 ft (1.8 m) should be right for most garden birds.

With the increase of interest in birds, the habit of feeding them at car parks and lay-bys has grown. Birds ranging from chaffinches to mallards may be seen wandering around the cars in the former. While at lay-bys, particularly when close to woodlands, tits, nuthatches, wrens and other species will come to food placed either on the ground or a wall top. For these places a car is the ideal hide. Although you will be working at fairly short range, the technique will be as described in the section on big-game photography (page 30)—though, of course, the engine will not be running.

Another way to photograph feeding birds is to set up a hide on the edge of a marsh, lake or sewage bed, where numbers of birds are known to feed. A single-lens reflex camera is necessary for this type of photography. In my opinion a 300 mm lens on a 35 mm camera is the most useful. The hide and

This common sandpiper on migration in England was photographed from a hide by the wait-and-see method. *Nikon SLR, 300 mm lens, 1/250 sec, f11, Tri-X film developed in Microdol-X.*

camera are set up as for a drinking place. There should be enough scope for reasonable movement of the lens, not only sideways but also to a lesser degree, up and down.

When you are settled behind the camera, it is possible to pick up the birds that are approaching in the viewfinder. Keeping them in the frame, you can then focus and expose when they are close enough. There will seldom be time to tighten both the pan and tilt movements of the tripod head. The pan movement should be adjusted so that it can be turned slowly without play, then the handle of the tilt screwed to within half a turn of the lock position. Holding the handle, you can keep the bird in the viewfinder and, if it stops within range, give the handle the final half turn and fire the shutter. Even if there is not time to do this, the rather tight settings and your hand steadying the tilt will reduce the risk of camera movement.

Even a 1/250 sec will not prevent parts of the image of a moving bird being blurred on the film. Therefore, you should only make exposures when it is fairly static. If the bird does not hesitate or stop, aim at photographing it when it has both feet on the ground. Where there is glutinous mud, as was the case when I photographed the common sandpiper on page 52, the bird's movements are slowed down. If working at a place where migrant waders gather in autumn, keep an identification list of your exposures. At that time of the year, the plumages of several species are somewhat similar and they are difficult to identify in a negative and, in certain postures, on a print or transparency. From time to time there are arguments in the ornithological press as to whether a photograph is correctly titled. What has sometimes happened is that the photographer has taken pictures of a rare species on the same film as some of a somewhat similar but commoner relative. When making prints he has mistakenly used a negative of the latter; this would not have happened if a record of exposures made had been kept.

Another way to photograph birds away from the nest is to take pictures of them resting at high tide. To do so, not only is it necessary to know where they roost, but as in many cases the place is on land that is surrounded by the incoming sea, a good knowledge of the local tides is essential. There is little to be gained by setting up where you will be washed off at high tide. Even with some knowledge and sound local guidance I have had the waves lapping the hide front at the peak of the tide. As there was higher ground behind, the only danger I was in was that I may have had to get out and disturb all the birds. Conditions vary from place to place, but where the land rises from a flat expanse of beach, all photographic preparations should be complete and the hide occupied while the edge of the incoming tide is a good distance away. If, when fairly close, the birds see any movement on what will soon be an island, they will choose another place to roost. The preparations are as for photographing birds on a marsh or sewage bed except that if you are on rock it is difficult to ensure the tripod's steadiness. If the tripod has stays restricting the outward movement of the legs, fix them at their widest. Where these are not fitted, the legs should be prevented from slipping outwards by connecting them together with cord. Then, in a sling suspended from the top, place a fairly heavy stone, keeping it clear of the ground; this will steady the tripod, particularly if one or more of its feet are resting on uneven parts of the rock.

As the tide rises, more and more waders are washed off the sandbanks and large flocks of them swirl around like smoke in the sky. When they decide to alight, the population of a large area descends on to the small roosting islands. Their arrival can be quite spectacular, the birds pouring down like grains of wheat from a sack. At first there is considerable jostling for a place and small groups may depart or land, but soon many are asleep with their bills tucked under their back feathers. As soon as the active birds are close enough to make

Golden eagle, taken from a hide on a cliff edge some 18 feet from the nest in Scotland. *Stand camera, 250 mm lens, c.1/10 sec, f22, P1200 plate developed in Azol.*

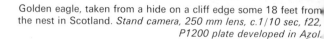

pictures, photography can start; shots of them can be taken on what have become isolated rocks and, finally, exposures can be made of them sleeping around the hide.

Play-back Technique

For hundreds of years hunters have imitated the calls of birds to bring them within range of their weapons or traps. In America, a local boy called down a screech owl to a tree within a few yards of the porch on which we sat and, in Britain, I have known a tawny owl act in a similar way when its call was imitated. Occasionally, birds have been brought to within range of the camera by this method. With the introduction of magnetic tape upon which songs can be recorded, it became possible to attract many species close enough to photograph them. This is a highly specialised branch of bird photography and, in addition to knowing the techniques of recording and photography, you need to know a good deal about bird behaviour.

The usual practice is for the photographer to prepare a recording of the song of a species of which photographs are required. This can be done in the field and then edited to make sure the song is repeated frequently. A photographer and a recordist may work as a team. Remember that copying from commercially produced material without permission is likely to contravene the copyright laws. The recording is then played to several singing birds of the species, and it will be found that certain individuals will react in the desired way. Once one of these is discovered, a perch can be placed in the area within which it is singing and the recording played close to it. The aim, of course, is to photograph the bird that alights upon the perch.

Very long focus lenses are used. Frank Blackburn, who has produced some magnificent pictures by using this method, recommends 500 mm–1000 mm lenses with a 35 mm camera. Much of his work is done without the use of a hide, but when he is working with birds that have rather a weak reaction to what must sound like an intruder, he finds one necessary.

As with all photography in the breeding area, care must be taken when this method is used. If the male is subjected for too long to the voice of a competitor that he cannot drive away, the pair bond may be affected. This is only a short outline of the method and anyone wishing to use the technique should first read what Frank Blackburn has to say in *Natural History Photography* published by the Academic Press.

Birds at the Nest

No branch of nature photography requires more skill and care than this. The bird's natural instinct to return to its eggs or young is strong and it is this that is relied upon to bring it back, even after a hide has appeared close to the nest. Not only is it unethical to put the birds under undue pressure, but to do so reduces the photographer's chance of success. Frightened birds may desert, but even if they come to the nest their attitudes are strained. Also, they may feed the young from the back of the nest, with only their heads showing above the rim. If you contemplate photographing a rare species—and you should have considerable experience of photographing common birds at the nest before you do so—first find out whether it is protected by law. It may be possible to obtain a permit to photograph, but in some cases protection will be absolute.

Without a Hide

Some birds, particularly sea birds that nest on oft-visited islands and others in remote places where man is rarely seen, will allow a close enough approach to be made for photographs to be taken without a hide. Many species of sea birds are colonial and pictures of the colony as well as of individuals should be taken. Pictures of the colony can often be taken with the standard lens of the camera.

Colonies nesting on cliffs make impressive pictures and can be photographed with almost any camera, as

▶

an examination of the technical details underneath the pictures in this book will show.

When it comes to photographing pairs at their nest, many of the cliff nesters will allow a photographer to get quite close. The photograph of kittiwakes at the nest on page 57 was taken with a

Two species that frequently nest adjacent to each other on narrow ledges on the English coast are kittiwakes and guillemots, stalked for this photograph. *Folding camera, 80 mm lens, 1/50 sec, f8, Tri-X film developed in Azol.*

Mamiyaflex. Reflexes are quicker to use than stand cameras and one can certainly get more—not necessarily better—pictures in a given period.

Kittiwakes make attractive pictures and it is sometimes possible to photograph them from the opposite side of a gully. In their first plumage the young have different markings to their parents. If you can find fully feathered nestlings alongside their parent,

interest is added to the photograph. The auks vary in their nesting habits. Guillemots lay their single eggs on narrow ledges, razorbills may also do the same but usually they prefer to deposit them beneath an overhang or more often in a cavity. Fortunately razorbills frequently stand about outside the holes and both species can be photographed on the ledges. Puffins and black guillemots lay their eggs where they cannot be seen, the first at the end of a burrow the second amid rock tumbles. To photograph them at the entrances of their homes a hide would be needed, but fortunately both species are often to be found in groups on rocks by the sea and are easily stalked. The eider duck, which nests on or by the shore, is a close sitter and sitting birds of this species may be photographed quite easily.

Some species of game birds and waders will continue incubating when one is quite close, but usually their crouched positions convey that they are aware of man's presence. That is also often the case with the occasional willow or reed warbler that will allow itself to be photographed without a hide being used.

With a Hide

To photograph birds at the nest, the first requirement is that a nest should be found. With species that breed in colonies, as do many seabirds, rooks herons and egrets, this is no problem. However, if you wish to take picture of such birds as warblers finches and larks, only with knowledge of nesting habits or with the help of someone who has, will you get to first base. If you do require assistance be very careful whom you ask for help. It is essential to keep disturbance near the nest to the minimum, and although small boys may be good nest-finders they are apt to tell their friends what they have found and even show them the nest. In a very short time the news has spread like the ripples made by a stone thrown into a pond, and even if the eggs are not taken, vegetation is trampled. Offering rewards is not a good way. Sometimes the photographer has been

shown a clutch of eggs and paid a reward. Next day the eggs have gone; the following day he has been taken to a clutch in a different area and again has paid up. Again they disappear and another site is found.

Rewards were being paid on the same eggs that were being moved from place to place. Although not all gamekeepers have a wide knowledge of small birds they, and in some cases estate employees, are the

A bird of the dusk, the little owl will also hunt by day. From the expanded irises of the eyes it can be judged that this bird was active late at night. It was photographed from a hide in England. *Stand camera, 220 mm lens, one flash head, f22, Tri-X film developed in Microdol-X.*

people most likely to give genuine help. No more than you will they want the area invading, and the nests are likely to be away from public access.

Once you have found or been shown a nest, the first thing to decide is whether it and the site are photogenic. If they are, the introduction of the hide can start. This must be done gradually and the method will vary with the type of habitat. Impatience at this

Female Kentish plover, Denmark. Although this species was named after a county where it was once common, it now rarely breeds in Britain; the partial burying of the eggs is quite normal. *Stand camera, 220 mm lens, c.1/25 sec, f22, P1200 plate developed in Azol.*

stage can cause the birds to desert their eggs or young. With the waders, ducks, game birds and other species that have chicks that leave the nest almost immediately after being hatched, the best time to start is when the eggs have been sat for several days. By that time the incubation behaviour will be firmly established. Where the young are reared in nests, it is best to wait until they are three or four days old. With either type, avoid starting at the time when eggs are chipping or young emerging. This is a critical period and nothing should be done that will deter the bird from returning quickly to the nest. A short absence can jeopardise its chance of rearing its young.

If you wish to photograph birds nesting in open fields, on moorland or broad beaches, it is as well to let them first have a good sight of the hide at a distance that does not appear to threaten the nest. The hide should be started some fifty-five paces from the eggs of a large wader such as a curlew. It can be set up at working height and, when finished, it should be able to withstand any weather conditions, have a tight, non-flapping cover and be protected against animals, if there are any. Erect the hide as quickly as is consistent with security and, by restricting your activities to its immediate vicinity, avoid trampling down the surrounding vegetation.

When all this has been done, take cover a long way from the nest—preferably at a place from which you can retreat without the bird seeing you—and watch it back. If it is not on the eggs in about half an hour it is likely that there is something amiss. If the bird is aware of your presence its actions will betray the fact. Then there is nothing for it but to move farther away. With a good pair of binoculars I have watched a golden plover back to its nest from half a mile distant. If at the end of another half hour the bird is not on the eggs, the hide should come down. Should you wish to do so, the hide can be tried at a greater distance on another day.

Once the hide is accepted it should be left in

This goldcrest, photographed from a hide in England, illustrates the value of waiting for an attractive site. I found many unphotogenic nests of this species before discovering this fine example. *Stand camera, 220 mm lens, a combination of daylight and one flash head, f22, Tri-X film developed in Microdol-X.*

position for a day. After that it can be moved forward to within about twenty paces of the eggs, the procedures of the previous day being followed. If there is no difficulty at that distance, after twenty-four hours the hide can be put some 10 yd (9 m) from the nest. From there, after being in position a day, it can be placed in working position for the focal length of lens you intend to use. If you have taken care, watched the bird back after every move and created the minimum disturbance, the bird will have accepted the hide as part of the landscape.

In open woodland you can make a similar approach although the starting point—because of undergrowth and foliage—may not need to be so far away. A hide where the sitting bird cannot see it does nothing to prepare the way for a move forward. Find the maximum distance the hide can be seen from the nest, on the side from which the photographs are to be taken. It does not matter if part of it will be obscured by trees or bushes. If the distance is less than thirty paces from the eggs of a wary bird, start the hide at half the normal height. There will be little chance of watching a ground-nesting bird back to the clutch, but you will require to know whether the hide has been accepted. To help to establish this a straw can be laid on the eggs or where a bird going to the nest will disturb it. As certain species, particularly those that sit tightly, are slow at coming back to the nest after being disturbed, go right away and do not return for at least an hour.

When you visit the nest to check, do not approach from behind the hide, but choose a route that will allow you to cross the ground in front of it. Do not use stealth; but approach naturally, talking in a normal way if there are more than one of you. The two things likely to sap the confidence of a bird that has returned and is sitting are the impression of an attempt being made to take it by surprise, or the sudden appearance of someone close to it. Walk as if to pass the nest, but only as close as is necessary to see it. One of three things may have happened: the bird may be back and sitting; it may have come back and then gone off again at your approach; or it may not have returned at all. If the bird is there or the straw has been moved, just keep walking and do not return to the site until the next day. If not, feel the eggs and check whether they are warm enough to have been recently incubated. It may be that the bird has managed to sit without disturbing the straw.

What is done next, if the eggs have not been sat, depends on what type they are and the weather. In warm, dry weather, large thick-shelled eggs are safe for a couple of hours; in very hot or very cold conditions, this may not be so. If there is any doubt, the hide should be taken down, and, as the eggs may be fresh, a few days allowed to elapse before another attempt is made. If all has gone well the hide can be lifted to full height next morning and after another day moving up can be carried out as already described.

Some game and other woodland floor-nesting birds will allow themselves to be photographed without the use of a hide. Anyone who has compared photographs of them crouched on the nest, with shots of them standing over or approaching their eggs, knows why it is worthwhile to introduce a hide.

With the smaller birds that nest in bushes or holes in trees, less preparation is required. The more common of these are good birds for the beginner to start with. Some warblers, tits, finches, flycatchers and thrushes will, with more or less delay, accept a hide erected at working distance. Some time will certainly need to elapse before the birds return to the nest, and when they do they will show their nervousness. Birds of the same species vary widely in their reactions, and there is no guarantee that because one pair will face a hide they all will.

Rather than have the experience of sitting in the hide with birds continuously skulking around giving alarm notes, but not coming to the nest, it is better to prepare in advance. Remember that the callow young may only live an hour if they do not receive attention from the parents. On the afternoon of the day before it is intended to start photography the hide can be placed about one and a half times the working distance from the nest and it should be kept as low as possible. It is not wise to start or move any hide late in the day; a bird put off the nest at dusk may not return in the dark.

Starting early next morning, move the hide to working distance and leave it for an hour. You will not need to see the nest to check whether the birds are feeding the young. It will be enough to watch them approaching close to it with food and leaving its vicinity with excrement in their beaks. Apart from 'gardening', which will be described in the next section, you should then be ready to start photography. If the birds do not return within an hour of your entering the hide, there is something wrong and it should be removed.

When you build hides in trees or on water, the work should be done gradually and a time limit set for each day's activity near the nest. If everything is

The sparrowhawk and nest were taken from a hide 20 feet above the ground in a Scottish forest. *Stand camera, 220 mm lens, c.1/10 sec, f22, Tri-X film developed in Microdol-X.*

organised and prepared, a team can do a lot of work in half an hour. Even so, with the time spent in leaving and returning, the bird will be away from the nest for nearly three-quarters of an hour and that is long enough. Five or six days on that basis should be adequate for a tree hide or pylon, and three to four for a nest on water (page 27).

The advice on introducing the hide can only be guidance, as no two sites or pairs of birds are exactly alike. Until field experience has been acquired err on the side of caution and do not take any liberties. The survival of the adults and their offspring is more important than any photograph. Of recent years photography at the nest has been criticised, often by uninformed people, so in no circumstance do anything that will supply the critics with ammunition.

Gardening

'Gardening' is a word used by nature photographers to describe the opening up of a site so that whatever is being photographed can be clearly seen. It is necessary for the photography of free and wild animals, plants and birds. The minimum should be done, and tying, not cutting, should be the normal method of dealing with intruding vegetation. If the subject is in dense cover that would have to be removed to allow the photograph to be taken, do not attempt it.

Although over recent years there has been a gimmicky trend to have out-of-focus foregrounds in pictorial and commercial photographs, the nature photographer should do everything possible to avoid them. Therefore, when 'gardening' around a nest, make sure there are no branches or leaves nearer than the front of the depth of field. If there are any, they should be held with green garden twine in the plane of focus or out of the picture. The fastening should not show in the photograph. Always be extremely careful to avoid disturbing the supports of the nest when arranging the foliage.

Small nests on the ground amid grass are difficult to prepare for photography. To retain a natural appearance and at the same time ensure that stray grasses do not spoil the picture requires considerable skill and care. Large, old fashioned hairpins are extremely useful aids. Use them—or wires bent to the same shape—to secure grasses in position in small bunches. All that is required is for the pin to be looped over them and its two ends pressed into the ground.

At the end of the day's photography you should release all ties and allow the covering of the nest to spring back, or else place it back in position. It is then that the care taken in 'gardening' is repaid, for you can leave the site knowing that the nest is as well covered as it was before photography started. Cut branches should not be propped in position as additional cover for a nest; they can do more harm than good. Leaves soon wither and betray the presence of the nest to people and predators. The branches may also slip and prevent the parent brooding the young.

Photography

Once the hide is in position and the other preparations complete, photography can commence. The setting up of the camera and the focusing will be as already described for a perch at a drinking place. It is essential that there should be someone to assist—nature photographers often work in pairs and take turns in the hide. When all is secure the assistant walks away drawing attention to himself by whistling or talking. Some birds require two decoys to depart, but most are satisfied with one. To enter a hide without having a colleague to walk away is usually a waste of time, but worse than that there is a great risk that it will cause the birds to desert.

Once left, the photographer should keep movement and noise within the hide to the absolute minimum. Avoid clothing that rustles and squeaky seats. No part of the body should touch the cover. Do not take a photograph the first time the bird returns to the nest. If it is feeding young you will be able to

A redpoll photographed from a hide in England; an example of an attractive site carefully 'gardened'. *Stand camera, 220 mm lens, c.1/25 sec, f22, P1200 plate developed in Azol.*

get some idea what to expect at the next visit; if brooding or incubating allow it a few minutes to settle. When you make your first exposure on the second visit, watch the reaction. If this is marked, do not wind on the film at once, but sit quietly watching. Once the bird with young has gone to collect food, the camera can be set for the next visit. Unless the sitting bird is obviously disturbed, wind on the film after a few minutes. Some birds ignore small noises from the hide; others need to become accustomed to them gradually.

Before the decoy departs, decide upon a time for his return and for some emergency signal. Coming out of the hide without another person standing by can cause disaster, in the same way as entering it unattended can. In the normal situation your assistant's presence at a pre-arranged time will enable the hide to be vacated without disturbing the birds greatly. If anything does go wrong, such as wind blowing vegetation in front of the nest, the easiest way to summon assistance is to put a handkerchief out of the back of the hide. This can be seen from a distance and your assistant can return to put matters right.

With nests in holes, or on the ground in thick vegetation, it is often more realistic to photograph the birds on a natural or introduced perch. If they are using a natural perch on the way to and from the nest, a hide can be brought gradually up to it. The photograph of bee-eaters on page 15 was taken at a colony in Spain where the birds were perching on roots protruding from the bank. When a perch has to be introduced, it should be close enough to the nest for the birds to use it regularly. It should also look natural; unfortunately many bird photographers, some with considerable experience, do not seem to realise this. Time after time one sees good bird portraits ruined by unsuitable perches. In many cases the photographer has cut a stick from the nearest hedge, removed the side twigs and stuck it in the ground, oblivious to everything other than getting a portrait.

The perch in the photograph of the pied flycatcher on page 66 was introduced.

The Use of Flash

Flash, either bulb or electronic, with one head produces heavy shadows and if these are to be kept to the minimum the lamp must be close to the lens; this will prevent the shadows from being too large in area. This method has much to recommend it for work on nocturnal birds; see the picture of little owl on page 58. It can also be used as a fill-in light to illuminate the shadows created in sunlit sites. Most workers now use electronic flash with two heads for photographing birds at the nest. The normal set up is to have one head fairly close to the camera and above the level of the lens, and the second on the other side of it, but further from the nest. Only experience will enable you to judge the exact position. With black-and-white photography excessively even lighting produces flat results and gives the impression that everything is in one plane. When used close to the nest, electronic flash has the great advantage of allowing a small stop to be used to increase the depth of field. Remember that when flash is going to be used, dummy reflectors should be introduced slowly along with the hide.

For photographs of birds flying to or from their nests flashes of very short duration are required. To produce flashes of 1/6000 sec special circuitry is required and the equipment will probably have to be made to order or constructed by the photographer. Firing the shutter by manual means, because of the difficulty of judging the bird's position in space, is not satisfactory for this type of photography. A photo-electric cell and a lamp are arranged in such a way that the flying bird is likely to break the infra-red beam between them. When that happens, the camera and flashes are fired. There is a very slight delay and the bird will have moved nearer to the camera when the exposure is made. Some allowance can be made for this when focusing, but a very small stop should be used to give the maximum depth of field. This

This cock pied flycatcher was photographed from a hide in Wales; it is standing on an introduced perch. *Stand camera, 220 mm lens, c.1/10 sec, f11, Tri-X film developed in Microdol-X.*

method is ideal for photographing nocturnal birds, but considerable skill is required to avoid all-black backgrounds in daylight shots. Nature photographs should look natural and pictures of birds in the daytime brilliantly illuminated against a black background do not. For further details, circuit diagrams, and information about taking photographs of birds in flight by flash, read the section by Dr D. A. P. Cooke in D. M. Turner Ettlinger's *Natural History Photography* published by the Academic Press.

Birds in Flight—Daylight

Although some photographers specialise in taking pictures of birds in flight, there are many others who like to add variety to their collection of photographs as the opportunity occurs. There is no doubt that both groups will find single-lens reflex cameras, that can be used at eye level, ideal instruments. The focal length of the lens will vary considerably in accordance with the conditions, size of bird and the distance it is likely to be.

This storm petrel was photographed by the specialised ultra-fast electronic flash of Dr D. A. P. Cooke.

Large numbers of birds in flight can make spectacular pictures; those on pages 69 and 70 were both taken with the standard lenses. When working with a 35 mm camera in seabird colonies I find a 135 mm lens about right for the photography of single birds in flight, although the fulmar on this page was taken with one of 80 mm. Longer focus lenses are required when taking shots of small birds or birds at a distance. I have found one of 300 mm focal length very useful, but the longer the focus of the lens

As this fulmar, photographed in Shetland, was gliding, it was possible to use a slower shutter speed than if it had been beating its wings. *Retina III SLR, 80 mm lens, 1/500 sec, f5.6, Panatomic-X film developed in Microdol-X.*

he greater the difficulty of finding the bird through it and the smaller the depth of field at a given stop.

With helical focusing it is extremely difficult to focus on a flying bird and even with the Visoflex system, where pressure or the release of a spring-loaded trigger moves the lens much quicker, it is far from easy. Most photographers set the focus and let the bird fly into it. The image is watched on the focusing screen and the trigger is pressed fractionally before it becomes absolutely sharp.

Exposure determination can be difficult as birds may come from any angle. Take one or two light readings, and adjust the camera settings for the average of them; remember that a dark bird against a clear summer sky will require a longer exposure than a white one. Experience will teach how much,

Gannets circling their Scottish nesting rock on a suitable breeze. *Retina III SLR, 50 mm lens, 1/500 sec, f5.6, Panatomic-X film developed in D76.*

Hungry young swallows, England. Although it is usual to describe a swallows' nest as 'stuck on', there is often some projecting object like the nail shown in this picture embedded in the nest. *Stand camera, 220 mm lens, one PF5 flashbulb, f22, P1200 plate developed in Azo▸*

but for a bird like a cormorant, double will not be excessive. If the bird's wings are beating, exposures of longer than 1/500 sec are seldom satisfactory. Even for some comparatively slow-flying species, one can only get the wing tips sharp at 1/1000 sec if the exposure is made when they are at the limit of their upward sweep.

Steady panning is very important. I find this easier with the camera on a shoulder-pod. In fact one uses the camera rather like a gun. The bird is picked up in the mirror, and followed smoothly, the aim being a little in advance of it; the camera is not stopped at the moment of exposure but continues with its follow-through.

An evening shot of a Scottish nesting colony of black-headed gulls. *Mamiyaflex, 60 mm lens, 1/500 sec, f5.6, Tri-X film developed in Microdol-X.*

For flight photography it is often a case of finding a place where the bird will approach you rather than stalking it. Flight-lines to and from nesting colonies and roosts are fairly constant. If you have a place where there is some cover—in front of a tree trunk is better than being in the open—you are likely to have plenty of opportunities. As birds prefer to take off and alight into the wind, face down it if possible. Fairly close to a colony the birds will be at their lowest altitude and, in relation to the ground, slowed down by the wind into which they fly.

Gulls at nesting colonies, at seaside resorts and inland parks where they are fed, also at rubbish dumps, are good to practise on. They are not particularly shy, are fairly large, have white underparts and glide from time to time. Often where they are provided with food they will circle low before alighting and it is comparatively easy to keep them in the viewfinder until they come into focus. Because of the speed with which the tips of the wings move on the down and up strokes, a fast shutter speed is required to prevent them being blurred on the photograph. However, with good panning, a gliding bird can be photographed at 1/250 sec.

The best time to take these photographs is morning or late afternoon. At those times the low sun will illuminate the undersides of the birds. Some very fine effects can be obtained on colour film quite late in the day. On my transparencies of the black-headed gull colony on page 70 the birds are gilded by the rays of the setting sun. Unless you are looking down on the birds, as you do from the top of a cliff, avoid photographing them in the middle of the day. The shadows beneath their wings and across their bodies can then be unrealistically black in the photograph.

Completing the Series

Some workers like to show as much of the bird's life cycle as possible. The techniques already described are suitable for photographing them in summer and winter plumages. In addition, shots of the habitat, eggs and young add interest. These shots can all be taken with the camera's standard lens. When photographing the nest do the minimum of 'gardening' and trampling of the area close to it. Leave the nest covered and tidy. Avoid plan views of eggs or young. Your picture of a cup nest should include two or three whole eggs as well as parts of the others.

Recommended Reading

Wildlife Photography, Eric Hosking and John Gooders (Hutchinson).
Natural History Photography, Ed. D. M. Turner Ettlinger (Academic Press):
Section 5, A. Gilpin
Section 6, J. B. and S. Bottomley
Section 7, F. Blackburn
Section 8, D. and K. Urry.

PLANTS

No one has benefited more from the introduction of colour film than the plant photographer. It has enabled workers in this field to render correctly the lovely colours of flowers and fungi, as well as the more subtle tints of mosses and seaweeds. This has encouraged many who were not interested in taking pictures in monochrome to take up this most interesting branch of nature photography. However, there is still a lot of satisfaction in making good black-and-white photographs, and in spite of the forecast of some photographers, I think that monochrome photography has a long future.

Although plant photography has the reputation of being easy, one soon finds that knowledge, skill and judgment are required to produce worthwhile results. As with all types of nature photography it is essential to know your subject and to be able to find and identify the plants. Sound knowledge will also ensure that the right characteristics are shown in the photographs. The difference between an outstanding and a mediocre plant photograph is often the choice of the specimen or group portrayed, and the surroundings.

Because of its varied movements, which allows the photographer to correct verticals and ensure that the sharpest definition is where it is required, plus the benefits of larger format material, the stand camera is the best for taking plant photographs. Next comes the

single-lens reflex camera. Ideally, this should have a removable pentaprism that can be replaced by a hood, down which one can focus. Much of the work will be close to the ground. An alternative is a right-angle finder that can be fixed to the eyepiece; with this the camera can be vertical or horizontal and still allow the focusing screen to be seen from above.

For most plant photographs the lens can be the standard one for the camera. Unless you are using one of the specially developed macro lenses with their extensive focusing range, you will need extension tubes. Fortunately with this type of subject, there is plenty of time to choose the right length. Occasionally an isolated plant in a lovely setting may be found and a lens of about two-thirds the focal length of the standard one will enable the photographer to take a portrait and include the scenic background.

As small stops and long exposures will be normal, a tripod is essential. Even if flash is used, the focusing can be much easier if the camera is on a tripod and then you can hold the flash in any required position.

Fungi

Fungi are ideal subjects for the beginner; they range from micro specimens to large tree-growing species that would require the use of a saw or axe to dislodge. Some are brilliantly coloured and others

Fly agarics (*Amanita muscaria*) photographed by Heather Angel.

Two photographs by Anne Jackson: Great bindweed on the left and traveller's joy (old man's beard) on the right.

beautifully shaped. Plenty of time can be spent in choosing the specimen and viewpoint. Fungi are not moved by every breeze that blows as are flowers, and unless there is considerable movement in the surrounding vegetation, the lens can be well stopped down and long exposures given. The front edge of the nearest fungus can be focused upon, the aperture set to f16 or f22 and exposures made up to, and even over, a second. Such a combination should ensure good all-over definition and the sharp foregrounds that are desirable in all types of nature photographs.

Although autumn is the main season for fungi they are to be found all the year round. Some, like the razor strop *(Piptoporus betulinus)* that grows on birches, can be effectively photographed in winter.

Flowering Plants

Photographing flowering plants is rather more difficult, because of the risk of movement during exposure, and the technical problem of getting some of them to stand out from their backgrounds. Flash can obviate the first difficulty; however, it is often unnecessary and should be used sparingly. A series of pictures all similarly lit can be very boring. Furthermore, the illuminating power of the flash falls off rapidly and while the occasional well-contrived picture of a flower against an almost black background can be very effective, oft repeated uncontrolled nocturnality is not. The ring-flash is particularly good for small plants and limited areas, but it and the normal electronic flash are most useful when combined with daylight as fill-in lighting.

A windless day with the sun hidden by a light layer of cloud is ideal for the photography of flowers. The soft lighting enables the delicacy of the light-coloured petals and the shadowed foliage to be rendered without undue contrast. Unfortunately, few days are ideal and on really windy days flower photography is out of the question; but when there are only light breezes there is often a chance of doing

good work. I sometimes think that the screens recommended by some specialists of this kind of photography are more trouble than they are worth. My impression is that they create air currents that make the movement of the flowers unpredictable.

The lady's slipper orchid is perhaps Britain's rarest flowering plant and is protected by law. *Mamiyaflex twin-lens reflex, 60 mm lens, 1/30 sec, f16 on Tri-X film developed in Microdol-X.*

Although at first glance a flower may seem to be moving continuously, often because of a lull it will be still for about a second. Choose the plant you wish to photograph and do the minimum 'gardening'.

Limit the 'gardening' to removing or fastening out of the angle of view very light-coloured objects in the background, and to ensuring that no vegetation will blow across between the camera and plant. Then place the camera on the tripod in position. When everything is ready you can settle down, release in hand, and take photographs only when the flower is still.

Blackthorn, by Anne Jackson

In any country there are more species of plants than there are of mammals or birds, and there is an almost daunting amount of material available to the photographer. This being the case, many workers prefer to specialise in one family and make photographic records of all aspects of the plants within it. In a birdwatching society of which I am a member, a colleague decided that in addition to taking bird photographs he would concentrate on taking pictures of orchids. Others seeing his sets of slides in which there were transparencies of these lovely flowers started to do the same and now there is a thriving group of orchid photographers in the society.

When you work on one family of plants the slight differences between its members become important, and to collect anything like a representative series the photographer requires close-ups of them. It would be easy to find a lifetime's work in photographing one single family in all its detail. For example, in Britain there are some fifty-two species of orchid growing wild. This does not seem a large number to portray, but some are very rare and others very local. Although in most areas there are several species, to photograph them all will involve considerable travelling and searching. In addition, members of the same species can vary widely in colour and size. Often the differences in the flowers of two or more species are quite small and, to make matters more confusing, hybrids occur with some frequency.

From the above it will be obvious that to complete a thorough coverage, photographs of the habitat, group—if there is one—and close-ups of the flowers are required, in addition to the portrait of the plant. In the last, care should be taken to include the leaves. A ring-flash will be found to be most useful to photograph the detail of the flowers as it will illuminate the tubular parts.

To do a series of the type just described you need to know a great deal about the family of plants. Acquiring that knowledge, the planning of excursions

and the searches all add considerably to the pleasure of the photography.

Water Plants

Flowers growing in water may be photographed from the bank, from a boat or by wading. A long-focus lens can sometimes make the last two unnecessary. Where it is possible to work from dry land there is much to commend doing so; the tripod can be set up in a stable situation and then you can work in comfort. Another advantage is that the wave patterns created by wading or a boat can be avoided. Wave patterns can keep the plants moving for a considerable time.

Trees

It is far more difficult to take satisfactory photographs of trees and bushes than at first impression it appears to be. They are large, near-stationary, abundant, and require neither special equipment nor skill to portray adequately. The problem is that of finding an example that has not been hacked and maltreated, in a site suitable for photography. All too often when a well-proportioned tree is found there are pylons, power lines, ugly hedges or farm buildings that cannot be kept out of the picture.

When a suitable tree in a good situation is found, it is worthwhile to photograph it clothed in leaves in summer and again when these have fallen and the twigs are bare. In order to avoid distortion, to isolate the tree or to obtain a better viewpoint, it is sometimes an advantage to use a lens of two or three times the normal focal length. Additional photographs can be taken of its bark, leaves, flowers and fruits. For all of these shots the standard lens will be satisfactory. When you are taking pictures of whole trees, you will find that a 2X yellow filter will improve the sky tones in a monochrome negative.

Globeflower. With flowers that grow close together it is a good idea to have a photograph of a group in the series. *Nikon SLR, 55 mm lens, 1/15 sec, f16, Tri-X film developed in Microdol-X.*

This giant redwood, Wellingtonia, was introduced into Britain and planted in many parks that surrounded Regency Mansions. *Nikon SLR, 135 mm lens with 2X yellow filter, 1/125 sec, f8, FP4 film developed in Promicrol.*

Fruits and Seeds

A somewhat neglected branch of plant photography is the portrayal of fruits and seed-containers.

Whether the former are those of the blackberry, pomegranate, prickly pear or any other fruit-bearing plant, and the latter the dandelion's parachutes, the sycamore's spinners or the pods of plants from which the seeds explode, they are worthy of attention. Some are very colourful and all are interesting.

Techniques and methods of photography will vary considerably. For the spike of lords-and-ladies with its orange-red berries, the dandelion's spherical head of feathered seeds and similar plants they will be as already described for flower photography. However, for the fruits that grow higher above the ground a pentaprism is an advantage on 6 cm × 6 cm single-

Teazle, by Anne Jackson.

lens reflex cameras. 'Gardening' in bushes can be reasonably easy as branches can be tied back and will spring into position again when released. With trees, 'gardening' can often be reduced to the removal of a few leaves that would in any case be shed in autumn.

Lichens and Mosses

Probably because they are difficult to identify and lack popular names, mosses and lichens do not seem to have the wide appeal of other plants. This is a pity, for when examined closely they are most attractive and extremely interesting. In either black and white or colour they make very pleasing pictures. To obtain adequate detail, many of the smaller lichens and mosses need to be almost life-size on the negative or transparency. Long camera bellows in relation to the focus of the lens, or extension tubes are required. As there is a short lens-to-subject distance, the depth of field will be shallow. When choosing an area to photograph try to select one that is flat, for even at the very small apertures that are necessary any curvature can result in out-of-focus planes that will detract from the final result. Good photographs can be taken in daylight strong enough to cast shadows, but the exposures will be quite long. The rather low-powered electronic flash units that fit into the accessory shoe of the camera are useful for this type of work. At this short range the flash is far enough from the lens to throw narrow shadows and this will prevent the final result having a flat, uniform appearance.

Ferns

Although distributed widely throughout the world, there are only about fifty species of fern that grow in the British Isles. Some are rare, and one is found only in the Channel Islands where it is not uncommon. In size they vary from about 1 in (2.5 cm) to 6 ft (1.8 m) in height. They are to be found in woodland, on rock faces and in the crevices of limestone pavements.

Photography is as for other plants except that ferns do not produce seeds, but instead have spores growing on the backs of the leaves. These appear along the leaf edges in late summer and autumn. Photographs showing them are easily taken in

Toothwort, by Anne Jackson.

controlled conditions. One good way to collect outline pictures of single leaves of different species does not even require a camera. First, select an open leaf about 8 in (20 cm) long; in the case of large leaves, a piece of that length from the tip will do. Then, in a darkroom lay the leaf on a piece of bromide paper, with a sheet of glass on top to hold it flat, and expose it to light. When the paper is developed it will be black except for the crisply defined white silhouette of the leaf.

Alpine clubmoss, *Lycopodium alpinium,* photographed in North Wales by Michael Proctor.

◀

The spores on the underside of a leaf of the *Polypody* fern, England. *Nikon SLR, 50 mm lens, 1/10 sec, f16, Tri-X film developed in Microdol-X.*

The silhouette of a *Polypody* fern taken without a camera.

Seaweeds

Around the coasts there are many species of sea weed. These can be very photogenic. Again, the standard lens of the camera will be found to be adequate for most situations. A polarising filter is a very useful, but not essential accessory. With it, surface reflections on the water can be obviated, but exposure is increased. When photographing sea weed in rock pools without a polarizing filter considerable care will be needed to avoid such reflections. The judicious use of an umbrella can often solve the problem. Calm days should be chosen as ripples can ruin the photograph. At low tide some seaweeds can be photographed clinging to out-of-the-water rocks. This should be done while the sea weeds are still wet, as this will show the typical surface texture. Avoid bright sunlight as this multiplies and extends the highlights, resulting in contrast and loss of texture. Light conditions by the sea are usually good, and for pictures of large areas the camera may be held in the hand, but for the short-range shots I would recommend a tripod.

Especially when photographing seaweeds under water, it is an advantage to know that the camera is focused, the shutter set, and then you can relax and wait for the right moment to expose.

Recommended Reading

Natural History Photography, Ed. D. M. Turner Ettlinger (Academic Press): Section 12, Michael Proctor.

Wild Flowers, John Gilmour and Max Walter (Collins).

British Plant Life, W. B. Turril (Collins).

Wild Orchids of Britain, V. S. Summerhayes (Collins)

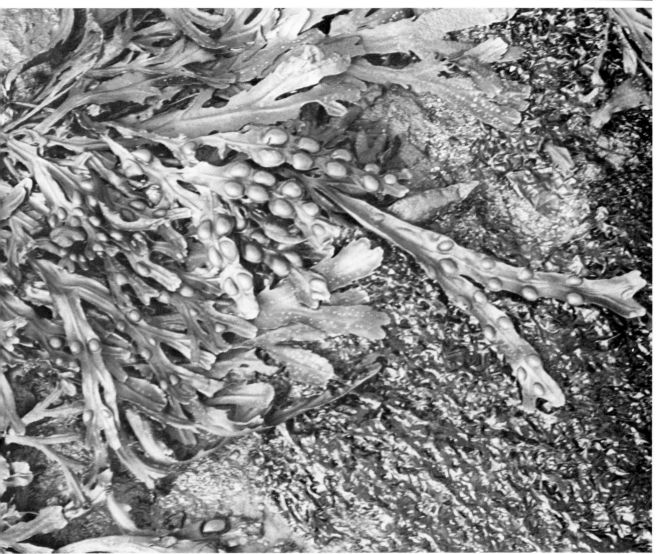

his bladder wrack, one of the commonest of the English seaweeds, was photographed above low tide level. *Nikon SLR, 50 mm lens, /125 sec, f16, Tri-X film developed in Microdol-X.*

INSECTS

With stand cameras and the clumsy reflexes that were in use prior to the introduction of the smaller modern single-lens models, few photographers took pictures of wild insects other than resting moths. Most of the latter are night-flying and rest on trees, walls or fences during the day. The great problem was that it was impossible to know where daylight-flying insects would alight, therefore you could not prepare to photograph them. When they did settle it was seldom long enough to allow the camera to be brought into use. One worker I know used to focus his field camera on a flower upon which he had placed a spot of honey and then wait. He did get some good photographs of butterflies, but only of a very limited number of species. In those days most of the best work was done indoors with the insects under control.

With the introduction of the smaller-format reflexes, stalking free and wild insects became a reasonable proposition. Now, in any set of competition or exhibition nature photographs—particularly when they are colour transparencies—a good proportion will be of insects. Most will have been taken in the wild, but, particularly for completing life histories, there is still a considerable amount of 'studio' work done.

The pattern of the beautiful golden Y moth blends with its surroundings (England). *Nikon, 50 mm lens, two flash heads, f16, FP4 film developed in Promicrol.*

Moths—Free

Although there are likely to be thousands of moths resting during a summer day on the trees and undergrowth of a comparatively small wood, the main difficulty for the inexperienced nature photographer is to find one to photograph. Therefore, as always, knowledge of natural history is more important than the more readily acquired photographic skill. Once the moth is found on some trunk, branch or wall that is not too high, the rest is easy and almost any camera that can be focused visually will do. When the insect is on the bark of a stout

The swallowtail is one of the butterfly species that rests with its wings open (Corsica). *Pentax SLR, 135 mm lens, 1/125, f8, Tri-X film developed in Microdol-X.*

tree or a mossy wall, movement should not be a problem. The camera, on a tripod, can be focused, the lens stopped down and quite a long exposure given; but if this would produce a result with too little contrast, flash can be used. Moths hibernating in caves also make very satisfactory pictures, but there some form of artificial light is required. I have seen extremely good black-and-white photographs where the only illumination came from a hand torch, and others where a short length of magnesium wire had been burned to provide the necessary light. Of course, a small electronic flash accessory is more convenient. Precautions and techniques similar to those recommended for the photography of hibernating bats in similar situations are suitable.

Butterflies—Free

Because of their bright colours and lovely shapes, butterflies are attractive subjects for both colour and black-and-white photography. With a single-lens reflex camera and patience, many species can be stalked successfully. With a 35 mm format camera I have found lenses of focal length from and including 50 mm to 135 mm to be the most useful. With most of them, extension tubes or bellows are required. When an opportunity for photography occurs, first focus the camera on some object of approximately the same size as the butterfly to be stalked. Then take an exposure reading of the vegetation, at the same angle from which you plan to take your picture. You can then commence your stalk.

Move slowly, avoiding any branches which, if touched, would swing about and disturb the butterfly, and make sure that your shadow does not fall upon it. When you are close enough to take the photograph without again moving your feet, find the insect in the viewfinder and move the head and body until it is sharp on the focusing screen, then press the release. If your camera has through-the-lens metering, check the exposure before taking another

Resting with closed wings is this grayling butterfly photographed in Sardinia. *Pentax SLR, 135 mm lens, 1/125 sec, f16, Tri-X film developed in Microdol-X.*

photograph. When you are close to the butterfly do not make any abrupt movements. If, because of the lens tubes or bellows, the automatic stopping does not work with through-the-lens metering, when the butterfly is in focus the lens can be stopped down until the exposure is right and then the exposure made. Without such metering, in spite of the reduced light, it is advisable to carry out the stalk with the lens already stopped down. That will avoid having to turn the camera to set the aperture with the risk of disturbing the insect.

Shutter speeds will require to be fairly fast to avoid subject or camera movement, but you must use a small enough aperture to get an adequate depth of field. Usually you have to compromise, but even in good conditions exposure times of 1/60 sec for the 50 mm lens and 1/125 sec for the 135 mm lens are about the minimum likely to give good results. Fortunately, butterflies usually choose the bright days on which to be active, so the light is likely to be good. Windy conditions should be avoided at all costs. There are enough problems without having to deal with an insect that moves in and out of focus on swaying vegetation.

Although lenses of longer focal length can be used successfully to photograph butterflies in the wild, I only use one when the insect proves to be very difficult to stalk. With them it is harder to avoid unsatisfactory backgrounds, the height of viewpoint is limited when compared with that of the shorter-focus lenses, and they are more difficult to hold steady.

Moths and Butterflies—Controlled

Most of those who specialise in insect photography like to produce life histories. Although both larvae and pupae can be photographed in their natural surroundings, to take pictures of the very small eggs one requires controlled conditions. Many workers prefer to photograph the whole life history indoors; this method does ensure having a perfect insect for the final stage. Many species are quite easily reared and the equipment is not expensive. However, as the range of plants on which the caterpillars of different species feed varies and in some cases is limited to one, a basic knowledge of entomology is required.

The rearing boxes do not need to be large, but should admit plenty of light and air. A box 8 in (20 cm) wide, 4 in (10 cm) deep and 12 in (30 cm) high, with a glass front that can be removed for the changing of food and cleaning, is about right for most species.

Air holes drilled in the top should be covered with fine net; this will let the air in and prevent the larvae escaping. For moths that pupate below the ground a layer of earth about 1 in (2.5 cm) thick should be spread on the bottom. To keep the food plants fresh the stems can be in a bottle of water, but they do require to be packed around with cottonwool to prevent the caterpillars being drowned. With very small larvae a smaller box will be more convenient.

You will not only need the boxes and the camera, you will also need either flash or photoflood as well as a narrow-necked bottle or something similar to hold the branch upon which the larvae or pupae will be photographed. If you use a bottle, partly fill it with water and put inside it the stem with a strip of lead wrapped around its lower end.

To photograph eggs, a camera with a long bellows extension and a very short-focus lens is ideal. Many eggs are so small that they need to be photographed at magnifications of from four to ten times. Many 35 mm camera can be used with microscopes or have special lenses and fittings for this class of work; however, this is not always the case. As there is a very shallow depth of field, the stops require to be small and the exposures long. The camera and subject must be rigid. To bring out the details and textures of the eggs, the lighting should not be too flat. The lamps can be moved around until the desired effect is seen on the focusing screen. When the photograph is actually being taken it is advisable to keep the room illumination very low. The shutter should be set at *time* and when the release is pressed, allow a short pause so that any vibration can settle, before the lights illuminating the eggs are switched on for the time of the required exposure. When these are turned off, the shutter can be closed. As exposures are at first a matter of trial and error, it is advisable to make the first series of tests on black-and-white film. It is easy to allow for the different film speeds of colour material when the correct exposure for a standard arrangement has been decided.

Privet hawkmoth caterpillar (*sphinx ligustri*) eating egg shell seconds after hatching, photographed by Heather Angel.

Larvae change their skins as they grow and in some cases their appearance changes with the shedding of the old skin, so it is an advantage to have photographs of them at each stage. It is comparatively easy to encourage the larvae on to a suitable branch or plant, and as they are not par-ticularly fast-moving, photography presents no real problems. The background should be some distance from the subject to avoid shadows being cast upon it. Once a satisfactory arrangement has been achieved, it and exposures can be near standardised, as only slight variations of the lighting will be required.

Whether flash or photofloods are used, two sources are needed to give good modelling in simulated daylight. With flash, colour film should be of the daylight type. It is possible to use the same with photofloods, but a conversion filter will be required and this will increase the exposure time. Alternatively, a film made for exposure in artificial light can be obtained. Photoflood exposures in the order 1/4 sec or even faster should be possible, but times will vary in accordance with the film speed and camera

Elephant hawkmoth photographed under controlled conditions in the daytime when moths can be quite docile. *Nikon SLR, 50 mm lens, two EF flash heads, f16, FP4 film developed in Promicrol.*

distance. With such slow exposures, photographs can only be taken when the subject is still and anyone doing this type of work regularly will find the low-priced, small, transistorised flash heads useful. At the distances involved their power is adequate.

All the cameras described in the section on equipment are capable of producing good results, but for this type of studio work, a stand camera with roll-film holder is perhaps the best.

When the larvae pupate they will do so on the food plants or on twigs put in the rearing box for that purpose. If the pupae are on food plants, photography cannot be delayed for too long as a plant in water is likely to droop fairly quickly. Photographs are taken in the same way and with the same apparatus as those of the larvae.

Often, when it is nearly time for the butterfly to emerge, there is a change of colour to be noticed on the pupa. If it is convenient to leave the photographic equipment in position it is advisable to assemble it, so that when the first sign of an insect emerging is noticed, photography can start. Otherwise, make sure that everything required is at hand and can be quickly arranged. The series can start with a photograph of the freshly emerged butterfly with its soft, limp wings wrapped around it. As the insect moves its hold on the chrysalis, so that the wings may hang clear of any obstruction, other opportunities occur. When the blood is pumped into the wings they begin to stiffen and dry out. About an hour after emerging, the butterfly is ready for its first flight. The photographer has in that time had chances of portraying it at all stages, from being a bedraggled creature to becoming a lovely one.

The methods and equipment as described for larvae are suitable, and in the early stages of the emergence, electronic flash is most useful.

For anyone who, for physical or other reasons, cannot pursue nature photography in the countryside, rearing and photographing butterflies at home is a fine substitute. Eggs, larvae and pupae can be bought from dealers and now those of many exotic species are available. Apart from the collection of plants for food, all the work could be done from a wheel chair.

Specimens caught out of doors and brought to the studio for photography usually settle down fairly quickly, and some females will lay eggs on suitable plants. As with bats and for the same reasons, the room in which they are photographed should have the minimum number of possible hiding places. You

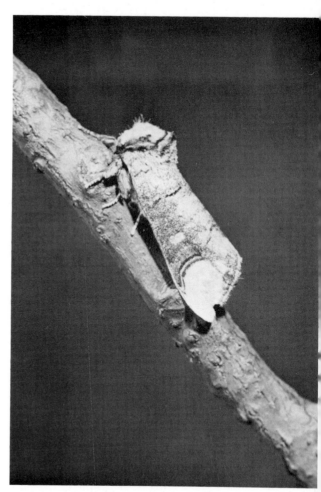

Two stages in the life-history of the buff-tip moth: on the left the caterpillar; on the right the moth itself. Both were photographed under controlled conditions. *Nikon SLR, 50 mm lens, two EF flash heads, f16, FP4 film developed in Promicrol.*

Dew-spangled hawker dragonfly photographed by John Armitage.

Darter dragonfly on cotton sedge, by John Armitage.

will need care and patience to get the insect into the desired position. Some butterflies normally rest with their wings closed; others will spread them when photofloods are switched on, just as they would in sunlight. As the photofloods have a very short life if used at full power, it is as well to have a rheostat or a series-parallel switch in the lighting circuit. You can then reduce the current until the photofloods are required for the actual exposure.

Dragonflies

As they have keen eyesight and frequently alight on plants growing out of the water, dragonflies are more difficult to stalk than butterflies. The larvae live under water and as the life histories of dragonflies are as interesting as those of butterflies, the photography of them will be dealt with in the aquatic-life section of this book.

Whether photographing wild dragonflies or portraying them in controlled conditions, you should use the same equipment and methods as for butterflies. I have already mentioned the difficulties of stalking, but with knowledge, experience and patience, good photographs can be obtained. It may be of interest to note that one of the best collections of photographs I have seen of dragonflies in the wild state was taken with a very simple camera by an extremely knowledgeable naturalist.

Rearing these insects is not particularly difficult if you have an aquarium, but it may be necessary to catch some to take controlled photographs. A butterfly net can be used to catch them. Care must be taken to avoid damaging the captive dragonflies and they should be released in their natural habitat when photography is completed.

Bees and Wasps

Usually it is possible to photograph these out of doors and in a free state. Many will be found visiting flowers, and others are partial to rotting fruit. These insects are more approachable than butterflies, but as their average size is much smaller, the camera should be closer to them. This, of course, involves longer camera extension, by either tubes or bellows. In other respects the photography is as recommended for butterflies.

Some wasp species build elaborate nests that are sometimes suspended from tree branches. These are well worth photographing, but any 'gardening' can be quite exciting! As soon as a branch directly connected with the nest is touched, out comes an angry swarm of wasps. Fortunately all the species I have photographed—unlike bees in similar situations—have not pursued the cause of the disturbance. A quick dash of some ten yards has been enough to take me outside the area of hostility.

Sites vary considerably; some nests are under conifers, where the light is so poor that flash is essential, others are in situations where they can be easily photographed by daylight. In addition to the colonial wasps, there are many solitary species with very different breeding cycles. Some lay their eggs in tunnels in the ground, others make little clay bowls on plant branches, stock them with tiny caterpillars as food for the grub, then suspend one egg above them before sealing the container. Many plant galls are the result of wasp eggs being deposited.

As with wasps, the habits of bees vary from colonial to solitary. A bumble bee's nest—roughly the size of a cricket ball—is usually sited in a cavity in the ground or a rock face. Some other species nest in

tunnels; those of the leaf-cutter bees are usually in wood and lined with sections of leaves.

For the photographer who is prepared to specialise there is plenty of opportunity for breaking new ground in the photography of wasps and bees.

This wasps' nest was at the side of a forest ride in England. The inhabitants resented intrusion! *Nikon, 135 mm lens, 1/60 sec, FP4 film developed in Promicrol.*

Beetles and Bugs

Beetles, the world's most numerous group of animals, are to be found in almost every type of habitat, and in practically every country. They range in size a great deal and in Great Britain the largest is about $2\frac{1}{2}$ in (6.5 cm) in length, and the smallest some $\frac{1}{25}$ in (1 mm) overall. Many are beautifully coloured, whilst shapes are very varied. Some alight on flowers, others feed on rotting wood and many are scavengers. If diligently searched, an area of woodland floor some ten yards square can yield a hundred different species.

Bug is the name rather loosely applied to insects that do not fly frequently and that have beak-shaped mouths. In body shape they vary from the broad shield bugs to the slender waterskaters. The two

A migratory locust of a species that sometimes reaches Britain alighted on rocks close to where I stood in the Corsican countryside. *Pentax SLR, 135 mm lens, 1/125 sec, f16, Tri-X film developed in Microdol-X.*

groups include many photogenic species. Large species can be photographed in their natural haunts but for many of the smaller ones better results are likely to be achieved in controlled conditions. The methods described for butterfly larvae are suitable.

Wherever you are, in whatever country, there will be plenty of insects. In addition to the species mentioned, large grasshoppers can be stalked and by being prepared, one sometimes gets unexpected shots. The photograph of a praying mantis transferring food to its mouth, on this page, was taken on a walk along a Corsican lane.

Recommended Reading

Insect Natural History, A. D. Imms (Collins).
Butterflies, E. B. Ford (Collins).
Natural History Photography, Ed. D. M. Turner Ettlinger (Academic Press):
 Section 10, S. Beaufoy.

Praying mantis in the wild, Corsica. *Pentax SLR, 135 mm lens, 1/125 sec, f11, Tri-X film developed in Microdol-X.*

REPTILES, AMPHIBIANS AND FISH

All these groups offer plenty of opportunity to the photographer and among them there are many interesting life histories to be recorded. Although much of the work is best carried out with the creatures in aquariums or vivaria, there is plenty of scope for the photographer in the field.

Snakes—Free

Few creatures are more misunderstood and, therefore, more persecuted than snakes. The flickering forked tongue is used to pick up scent from surroundings and is not the stinging instrument it is often believed to be. Of the world population of well over two thousand species, only a comparatively small proportion is venomous. It is perhaps superfluous to point out that the photographer should be able to recognise those that are.

There is no doubt that the handiest camera for field work is a 35 mm single-lens reflex. The focal length of the lens used will depend on the type of snake being photographed and its approachability. When found basking in the sun, many species are not difficult to stalk. In some cases a tripod may be used, in others the camera will need to be hand-held. In the latter case exposures should be short enough to prevent camera shake. Focusing will be direct on to the snake. Although deaf, snakes can feel vibrations and move quickly if disturbed.

As they grow, snakes shed their skins in one piece. These are fragile and, photographed where left, make interesting and attractive pictures.

Lizards—Free

There are in the world about as many species of these as there are of snakes, but only one of them is really poisonous. One British lizard is legless, looks rather like a snake and is popularly called 'slow-worm'.

When photographing lizards I have found a 35 mm single-lens reflex camera with a 135 mm lens about right. For the smaller ones you will need an extension tube or bellows. One difficulty is to have, at the same time, a shutter speed fast enough for hand-held shots and an aperture small enough to provide an adequate depth of field. The lizard's long tail may curve either away or towards the camera and should be in focus.

Sunny days, when the reptiles bask on the warm rocks, are ideal for this type of photography. Lizards move quickly when disturbed and in order to stalk one, it is necessary to see it before it sees you. This is best achieved by moving around slowly in a suitable area. When you see one sunning itself, taking into consideration the direction of the light, approach it slowly in much the same way as recommended for butterflies. Sometimes you may disturb a lizard that darts away, but does not go into cover. If it has stopped in a photogenic place, allow it time to settle before commencing to stalk it.

For the family man or woman holidaying in southern Europe or places with a similar climate, the photography of lizards can provide pleasant inter-ludes. It can be carried out with the photographi[c] equipment that is normally carried on vacation, a[t] times when the rest of the family are on the beach o[r] resting.

A rock lizard stalked while it was basking in the Corsican sunshine. *Pentax SLR, 135 mm lens, 1/125 sec, f11, Tri-X film developed in Microdol-X.*

his chameleon, photographed in the Transvaal, was angry and many-coloured because it had just been attacked by a pair of weaver birds. *ikon SLR, 50 mm lens, 1/125 sec, f16, FP4 film developed in Promicrol.*

Toads often rest in holes during the day; this one was in Denmark. *Stand camera, 220 mm lens, 1/10 sec, f22 on P1200 plate developed in Azol.*

ewts or Salamanders

hese may be mistaken at first glance for lizards, but nlike those reptiles they do not have scales. Their kins are smooth and, in some cases, lumpy. They y eggs and pass through an underwater larval age before the eft leaves that element. The adults so go on to the land after the breeding season, but s they remain hidden in damp places during the day nd feed at night, there is seldom chance to photo- raph them except in controlled conditions. How- ver, if an opportunity of photographing one in a free nd wild state occurs, the fact that it has seldom been one is an added incentive.

rogs and Toads

oth lay eggs in water, those of the common toad eing in long strings, and from these tadpoles merge. Frogs of the same species will vary widely in olour; I have seen one bright red example of the ritish common frog, although this species is sually greenish in colour. Frogs prefer the wetter laces in which to live, while toads are more uggish than frogs and tend to stay in holes during e day. There are no real photographic problems, nd almost any camera that can be focused accurately nd reasonably quickly can be used to take photo- raphs of adults found in daylight.

ish

he opportunities of photographing fish in a natural ate are limited, but some work has been done in is field. Of freshwater species, salmon and trout ave been photographed successfully when leaping, s well as, along with a few other species, under ater. Some marine species such as blennies and obies have also been photographed in rock pools.

Photographs of leaping fish are usually taken when ey are moving up river to spawn. A fast shutter eed or the use of electronic flash is required to get a arp image and often the distance is too great for e last-mentioned method. Apparatus and technique

are much as for flying birds. Having decided upon the place from which fish jump most frequently, set the focus and take when one leaps in the right place.

Gamefish often spawn in extremely shallow water and are then reasonably good material for photo- graphy. So are marine fish and other creatures in the shallow rock pools left by the tide. These can be photographed with the same equipment and in the same way as recommended for seaweeds in similar situations.

Snakes and Lizards—Controlled

There are obvious advantages in photographing snakes, particularly venomous ones, in zoos. The main problem may arise from the glass, through which the photograph must be taken, being dirty or scratched. Lighting will almost certainly have to be flash, and care will be required to prevent reflections of the camera and hands appearing in the picture. As already mentioned (page 43), this can be avoided by fixing a black card, with a hole for the lens, in front of the camera. Lights should be positioned as shown on page 105. Some zoos have restrictions on photo- graphy, so it is as well to see whether they can be waived and whether extra facilities can be granted by the authorities.

The photography of lizards and small snakes can also be carried out in glass-sided vivaria as described for small mammals.

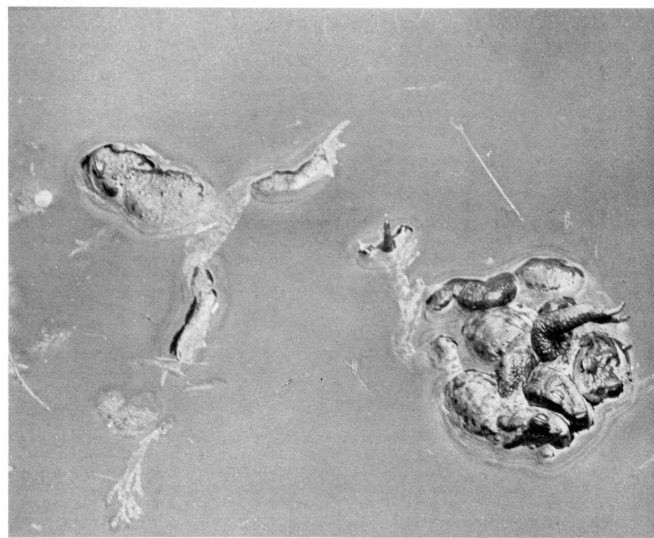

Common toads, England. Normally a single male toad clings to the female to fertilise the spawn, but occasionally—probably because of a shortage of females—several will do so. *Nikon SLR, 135 mm lens, 1/60 sec, f11, FP4 film developed in Promicrol.*

Newts—Controlled

These can be treated like lizards for the land phase of their existence, but otherwise they will be aquarium subjects.

Experience will teach you how much space to allow creatures being photographed in vivaria. Too much space may make it difficult to photograph the subject in the desired situation. Too little space often results in uncomfortable creatures and unnatural photographs. Let reptiles settle before any attempt at photography is made.

The lighting in the private aquarium was arranged to emphasise the under-body pattern of this male great crested newt. *Nikon SLR, 50 mm lens, two EF flash heads, f16, FP4 film developed in Promicrol.*

Unlike the male, the female great crested newt does not have a crest, although she is usually the larger of the two. *Nikon SLR, 50 mm lens, two E7 flash heads, f16, FP4 film developed in Promicrol.*

Photography in Aquariums

Photographs of natural-history subjects, covering a wide variety of species, can be taken in an aquarium. If this type of work is to be done regularly it is advisable to have keeping tanks in which the creatures can live and at least one tank for photographic use only. The size of the tank used for photography will depend on how large the creatures to be photographed are. It is easier to take pictures of the smaller ones in small tanks, than it is to divide off a large container.

Aquatic animals and insects are susceptible to changes of temperature and water conditions. Owing to the additives put into tap-water for various reasons, tanks filled with it should be allowed to stand for a day or two before live creatures are put in them. The water in the photographic tank should be mature and at the same temperature as that of the one from which the creature to be photographed is taken.

For various reasons algae form on the glass of keeping tanks, and in cleaning them off, the surface is likely to become scratched. It is on account of this and the need to keep whatever one is photographing in a workable area, that a studio tank is necessary. The front of this should be of undamaged plate glass to ensure good definition and the minimum of retouching later. A piece of clear plastic sheet to form a movable upright partition the length of the inside of the tank is also needed. In order that this will fit tightly in any position, without exerting undue pressure on the walls of the tank, it should have rubber strips at each end. With this, one can confine the animal or insect temporarily to the front of the tank and yet show the background in the picture. If this is fixed at an angle, the fish can be kept off the tank bottom if required.

The studio tank should be prepared well in advance, with a background of rocks or plants according to the species to be photographed. If rocks are used make sure that they are well washed. The partition should be inserted where required and the whole given a day or two to allow matter suspended in the water to settle and any air bubbles to escape.

The lighting used will depend on the subject and what one wishes to illustrate. To emphasise how the markings of a bottom-feeding fish blend with its background, or how some fish partially bury their bodies in the sand, top lighting, with the camera above the tank, is required. For pictures through the glass front of the tank the artificial lighting should be basically as shown opposite. According to the

Elevation for top and side lighting of aquarium

Plan of front lighting of an aquarium or vivarium

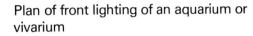

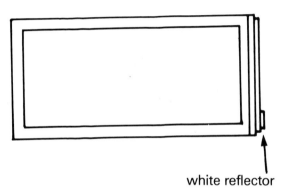

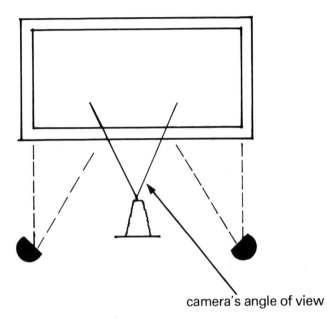

white reflector

camera's angle of view

Elevation of equipment for shallow-water photography

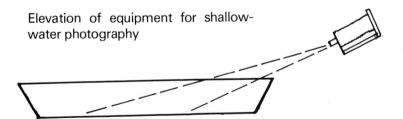

Photography in aquaria and shallow water

circumstances daylight, photofloods or flash can be used. As photofloods create heat they should be used at full power only for the period of the exposure and should be wired as described on page 93.

As the camera for this type of photography will b on a stand, any of the cameras described as suitab at the beginning of this book will give satisfactor results. The lens-to-object distance is in the photo

The roach—this one was photographed in a private tank—is a common fish of the middle stretches of British rivers. *Nikon SLR, 50 mm lens, two EF flash heads, f16, FP4 film developed in Promicrol.*

rapher's control, and it will, to a large extent, be the size of the species that will determine the focal length of the lens used. Unless you are attempting some special effect, it is a good idea to use the shortest-focus lens that will do the job in hand.

Insects in Aquariums

Those insects that live on the water's surface or surface plants will photograph best from above. Care will be required to ensure that there are no light reflections from the water within the camera's angle of view. The adults and the larvae of some species that live underwater can be photographed through the front. They can be in a fairly narrow space between the perspex and the glass, with one or two plants, a suitable background having already been arranged on the other side of the partition.

Dragonfly nymphs crawl up a stem until the fore-parts of their bodies are out of the water when the time for the metamorphosis to a perfect insect arrives. The emergence can be photographed in much the same way as that of a butterfly.

Amphibians in Aquariums

The aquarium is an ideal place in which to photograph toads and frogs laying eggs, newts in their sometimes brilliant breeding dress, and also the life histories from eggs to adult.

Fish in Aquariums

Apart from those from temperate climes, a wide range of tropical fish can be photographed in aquariums. Of course, the temperature in both keeping and photographic tanks must be correct for them. Many are very colourful and with the water plants well arranged behind them they make lovely pictures. Others, like gouramies and Siamese fighting fish, build bubble nests near the surface for their eggs. If after the eggs hatch one of the young falls out, it is usually caught by the guardian parent below and blown back into the mass of bubbles. Mouth-breeders carry their eggs around in their mouths and even the free-swimming young will retreat into the place they were hatched when danger threatens. To obtain photographs of these breeding habits it is necessary to keep the fish undisturbed in one tank for a considerable time before and during photography.

Portraits of individual fish of the smaller sizes can be taken in tanks that can be kept in a house, in the same way as those of aquatic insects. The tanks and the spaces between the plastic partitions and their fronts will require to be larger. However, for some of the larger fish one must go to a zoo. There, one will be almost certainly limited to the use of flash through the front of the tank and have the problems mentioned on page 43.

There are many other creatures, such as terrapins, that can be photographed in an aquarium in much the same way as the fish and insects. In one the whole growth of aquatic plants, rather than only the part above the water, can be portrayed and the difference between the leaves above and below water that occurs in some species can be shown.

Other Small Aquatic Creatures

Many small aquatic creatures can easily be photographed under controlled conditions in shallow water. The only additional equipment required is a large dish. Dishes used for developing enlarged photographs are ideal for this purpose and, as they are made in a variety of sizes, there is no difficulty in obtaining one to suit the subject.

First, the bottom of the dish is covered with sand, gravel or small rocks to match the normal surroundings of the creature to be photographed, and then filled with water. The dish should be on a firm table or bench, to prevent any small vibrations disturbing the surface of the water. After whatever is to be portrayed has been allowed to settle down, photographs can be taken over the edge of the tray. It is possible to use any of the cameras and forms of lighting already described.

There are several advantages of working indoors. It is easier and safer to set up photographic equipment on a bench or level floor than it is on slippery rocks or in shallow water; there are no wind-create surface ripples; and, whatever lighting is use reflections can be avoided or controlled.

Cameras and water—particularly when there salt in it—are best kept apart and I have found th

These beadlet sea anemones were photographed in a large photographic developing dish. *Nikon SLR, 50 mm lens, 1/4 sec, f16, FP4 film developed in Promicrol.*

method particularly useful for photographing sea anemones and small crabs, from rock pools and the shallow sea. Whatever is to be photographed, in some cases with a rock it is attached to, can be carried in a bucket filled with water in which it has been living, to a place suitable for photography.

Whether you work with freshwater or marine life there is no reason why the equipment should not be carried in a car and used in a building or shelter close to the source of supply. The creatures can then be photographed in water to which they are accustomed and returned to their natural haunts when photography is completed.

A Malayan angel fish taken through the double glazing of a tank on exhibition to the public. *Nikon SLR, 50 mm lens, two EF flash heads, f16, FP4 film developed in Promicrol.*

THE FINAL PICTURE

Whether the final result is to be a print or a transparency, there are a few basic requirements to which it must conform if it is to be worthwhile. To produce the right density in a transparency or the correct tonal range in a print, the exposure must be right. As colour plays such an important part in the identification of many species, it is more necessary that it should be correct in a natural-history photograph than in a landscape picture. In most cases it is desirable to have good definition over the whole of the creature or plant that is the main feature of the photograph. If, however, only part of it is being shown, for example, the stamens of a flower or the inner ear of a bat, the best definition must be on the area chosen.

Fashions in photography change and the consensus of opinion at the time decides what is considered to be aesthetically pleasing. Furthermore, individual tastes differ. At no time is the generally accepted standard inviolate and it is today's successful innovations that make tomorrow's range of acceptability. Unless some nature photographs are taken that do not fit within the normal pattern, we should be condemned to mere repetition.

While from time to time you can see very successful nature photographs in which the image of the animal or plant fills most of the picture area, or alternatively is quite small in an extensive landscape, in most cases it occupies between a third and a tenth of the print. The actual proportions are decided by the composition; although with a subject taken in the wild state, it is usual to include enough of the habitat to show that it is in its natural surroundings. However, it is the general practice to have a proportionally larger image of the creature or plant concerned on colour transparencies and on prints submitted for publication.

In addition to the whole of the main feature, it is an advantage to have the foreground of the picture crisply defined; if blurred it can form a barrier between the main subject and the viewer. Conversely an out-of-focus background enables the areas with good definition to stand out.

The attitudes of mammals and birds should appear reasonably relaxed and unstrained. Any excessive 'gardening' shows in the final result, and care should be taken that tied foliage or cut ends do not appear in it. There is little you can do about spots and scratches on transparencies, but you can make sure that all loose dust is removed from them before they are projected. It is very depressing to view a set of slides that look as though they have been stored in a vacuum-cleaner bag. A soft brush used gently will clean off dust. Do not wet the film unless it has already been splashed with liquid. If that happens accidentally, immerse the film in clean water, allow it to soak for about five minutes, then hang it in a dust free place to dry. Defects on prints should be spotted out with suitable watercolour.

To sum up: the aim is to present a recognisable picture of a creature or plant in natural-looking surroundings, without any indication of the photographer's presence.

Ancillary Photographs

It is easy to become so immersed in the photography of wild creatures that the taking of supporting photographs is overlooked. Whether one writes illustrated articles, lectures, or just keeps the pictures for one's own satisfaction, not having spent time and thought on completing the series of photographs is often cause for regret. Furthermore, it requires little extra effort to produce attractive pictures than it does to take records of no aesthetic appeal.

It may be thought that taking a photograph of a hide 'in situ' does not allow much scope for picture making. However, although the angles from which it can be taken may be limited, there may be a choice of distance that will allow the photographer to include or exclude desirable or unwanted features. The lighting can enhance or mar the photograph, so its effect should be carefully considered.

Photographs of the immediate surroundings, with actual site included, and a general landscape picture of the adjacent countryside are useful additions to any series. Often, when this type of picture is taken, the lighting is at least as important as the content.

For the photography of hides and the immediate habitat the camera's standard lens is usually quite suitable. When taking pictures of landscapes, a lens of longer focus will give a more pleasing perspective. For example, many photographers when taking photographs of open scenes use a lens of 80 mm focal length on a 35 mm camera, rather than the standard one of about 50 mm. For taking black-and-white pictures, except when trying to capture misty effects, a 2X yellow filter will improve tone values, particularly in the sky.

In addition to their direct interest, photographs showing equipment arranged for controlled indoor work can provide a valuable record of methods and techniques. With a few notes they can be an excellent guide, particularly when you want to repeat a set-up that has proved successful.

FIELD GUIDES AND SOCIETIES

If you are already a photographer and have recently become interested in natural-history photography, you will need to learn as much as possible about the particular branch of natural history that you have undertaken. Some of the information can be obtained from books. The first step is to learn to recognise the different species. In the last three decades many Field Guides have been published and for birds and mammals there is a near-worldwide coverage. All the other families mentioned in this book are reasonably well covered in the Field Guides of Europe and North America, but some parts of the world do not have such guides.

Field Guides are, as their name implies, books that can be easily carried in the field, and usually fit comfortably into a jacket pocket. Along with the pages of coloured pictures, they contain the basic information necessary to identify the species described. Until you are experienced, I would advise you to carry a guide dealing with the species you intend to photograph when working in the field. Space allows for only a more or less random sample of those available to be listed.

Field Guides to Mammals

A Field Guide to the Mammals of Great Britain and Europe, F. H. van den Brink (Collins).

A Field Guide to the Larger Mammals of Africa, Jean Dorst and Pierre Dandelot (Collins).

Field Guides to Birds

A Field Guide to the Birds of Britain and Europe, Roger Peterson, Guy Mountford and P. A. D Hollom (Collins).
The RSPB Guide to Birds, David Saunders (Hamlyn).
The Birds of Southern Africa, O. P. M. Prozesk (Collins).
A Guide to the Field Identification of the Birds of North America, Chandler S. Robbins, Bertel Bruur Herbert S. Zim and Arthur Singer (Golden Press New York).
Birds of the West Indies, James Bond (Collins).

Field Guides to Flowers and Plants

The Wild Flowers of Great Britain and Norther. Europe, Richard Fitter, Alastair Fitter and Marjori Blamey (Collins).
The Oxford Book of Wild Flowers, B. E. Nicholson S. Ary and M. Gregory (Oxford University Press)
The Pocket Guide to Wild Flowers, David McClintoc and R. S. R. Fitter (Collins).
Flowers of Europe, Oleg Polunin (Oxford Universit Press).

Flowers of the Mediterranean, Oleg Polunin and Anthony Huxley (Chatto and Windus).

A Field Guide to the Trees of Britain and Northern Europe, Alan Mitchell (Collins).

Beginners' Guide to Seaweeds, C. L. Duddington (Pelham Books).

Field Guides to Insects

A Field Guide to the Butterflies of Britain and Europe, L. Higgins and N. D. Riley (Collins).

A Field Guide to the Insects of Britain and Northern Europe, Michael Chinery (Collins).

Butterflies of Trinidad and Tobago, Malcolm Barcant (Collins).

A Field Guide to the Butterflies of the West Indies, Norman D. Riley (Collins).

Field Guides to Snakes

A Field Guide to the Snakes of Southern Africa, V. F. M. FitzSimmons (Collins).

European Snakes and Amphibians, Joachin Blum (Foules Spectrum Books).

Guides to Aquaria and Marine Subjects

Aquarium Fishes, Claus Payson (Hamlyn).

Pocket Guide to the Seashore, John Barrett and C. M. Yonge (Collins).

Photographic Societies

Mixing with others of similar interests widens your knowledge and this is particularly true for the photographer. There is no better way of keeping abreast with methods and techniques than being a member of a camera club or photographic society. Nature photographers are a minority group, but most photographic societies number one or two among their members. Most towns have at least one such society and some cities have several. In Britain the national body is *The Royal Photographic Society* and their headquarters are at 14 South Audley Street, London W1Y 5DP. They have recently formed a group — Heather Angel is its chairman—for workers in the natural-history field and meetings are held at the above address and in the provinces.

The other specialist natural-history photographic societies in Britain are portfolio circulating. Members receive a portfolio at monthly or two-monthly intervals, comment on each photograph in it and then place one of their own in a folder on which other members will write comments, before posting it to the next on the route list. There are societies for all types of nature photography and each is represented on the Executive of *The Association of Natural History Photographic Societies*.

The societies are:

The Zoological Photographic Club. The Hon Secretary is Mr D. Platt, Heathside, Tubney, Nr. Abingdon, Oxfordshire. This is the oldest of the societies. It is for prints — colour or black-and-white — and accepts photographs of animals, birds, insects and other forms of mobile wildlife. Controlled work is acceptable, but as is usual in these portfolios, it has to be declared as such.

The Nature Photographers Portfolio. The Hon Secretary is Mr A. Winspear Cundall, 8 Gig Bridge Lane, Pershore, Worcestershire WR10 1NH. There is one portfolio for prints and another for transparencies. The range of subjects circulated is similar to those mentioned above. Transparencies of all sizes are catered for in the transparency folio; the members of this folio are not required to be members of the print portfolio.

The Nature Photographic Society. The Hon Secretary is Mr E. A. Janes, 36 Little Gaddesden, Nr. Berkhamstead, Hertfordshire HP14 1PF. This society is for prints. These, in colour or black-and-white, can be of any type of natural-history subject. There has always been a strong contingent of plant photographers among its members. Of the print portfolios this is the most varied in content.

The Nature Stereoscopic Club has recently been revived and the Hon Secretary is Mr J. W. Bruce, 27 Glen Grove, East Kilbride, Glasgow G75 0BG.

As its name implies, the club is for those who take photographs in stereo. This method was widely used by early nature photographers and it is good to see a revival of interest in this satisfying process.

The United Photographers Portfolios (Natural History Colour Circle). The Hon Secretary is Mr N. A. Callow, 14 Avenue Elwers, Surbiton, Surrey KT6 4SF. This is for colour transparencies of any standard size and any natural-history subject. It has a membership active in many branches of natural-history photography.

The 35 Postal Club (Natural History Colour Circle). The Hon Secretary is Mr P. Nolan, 'Seven Stones', Upper Padley, Grindleford, Sheffield S30 1JA. As with the last-mentioned society, there is no restriction on subject matter other than that it must have natural-history content, but it is restricted to 35 mm transparencies.

Some of these societies ask for examples of an applicant's work before accepting him or her for membership, others do not.

Natural-History Societies

What has already been said about the advantages of being a member of a society is just as relevant for those interested in natural history as for those interested in photography. Most cities and towns have natural-history societies, some of them long established. During the winter, lectures on a wide range of subjects are arranged by them; in summer, outings to places of special interest are usually well supported.

With the ever-growing need for conservation more and more land is being taken over for nature reserves. This is done to preserve the creatures and plants, also to reduce the risk of their being adversely affected by developments or human pressures. Sometimes the pressure is physical, in the form of too many feet on the same piece of land. The local body most likely to have reserves is the County Naturalists' Trust. Before you visit a reserve for photographic purposes it is as well to know the restrictions, if any. If in doubt write to the Trust's secretary for permission to take photographs. Attitudes will vary, but unless photography is likely to cause disturbance, they are usually favourable; in fact the Trust may welcome copies of photographs for its own use.

National Societies and Associations

The Nature Conservancy, 19–20 Belgrave Square, London SW1X 8PY. This is a government department and those wishing to photograph birds on Schedule 1 of The Wild Birds Protection Act should apply to it for the necessary permit to do so.

The Royal Society for the Protection of Birds, The Lodge, Sandy, Bedfordshire SG19 2DL. The aims of this society are to protect birds in every possible way. Its activities cover a very wide field, ranging from owning and wardening reserves all over Britain to investigating, and when necessary prosecuting, offences against the Wild Bird Protection Acts. Photographs can be taken from some of the public hides on their reserves.

The Society for the Promotion of Nature Conservation, The Green, Nettleham, Lincoln LN2 2NR. This is the parent body of the County Trusts and is concerned with the conservation of nature in all its forms.

The British Trust for Ornithology, Beech Grove, Tring, Hertfordshire. This society was formed to further the study of birds. It organises enquiries into various aspects of bird life and it has produced a great deal of valuable ornithological information.

Mammal Society, Biology Department, Building 44, The University, Southampton SO9 5NH.

Botanical Society of the British Isles, c/o Botany Department, British Museum (Natural History), Cromwell Road, London SW7 5BD.

British Entomological and Natural History Society, c/o The Alpine Club, 74 South Audley Street, London W1.

British Herpetological Society, c/o Zoological Society of London, Regents Park, London NW1 4RY. A society with special interest in the reptiles of Britain and Europe.

Marine Biological Association of the United Kingdom, The Laboratory, Citadel Hill, Plymouth, Devon PL1 2PB.